Other books by Shannon Olson:

Non-fiction

It's Called a Trout Stamp Not a Food Stamp

Coming Soon.....

**I've Got Bugs Fly Tying Manual, Co-authored
with his wife, Jenny Olson**

Shannon James Olson

Ramblings of the Man Who Killed 1000 Ducks and 20 Friendships

....And that was just one season

Follow Shannon's blog at www.ivegotbugs.com
Or on Facebook at www.facebook.com/ivegotbugs

Acknowledgment

First I would like to thank God. Without him I would have never been able to enjoy the life and moments I have been blessed with. More importantly, I wouldn't have been able to survive most of them. I would also like to thank my parents for raising me to be who I am and to stand up for what I believe in. Then my kiddos, I have learned more from them than anyone else I have ever crossed paths with. The greatest gift a man could have is his kiddos. Then to all my friends, thanks for putting up with me and sharing some of the great and not so great chapters in this story we call life. Last would be a great big thanks to everyone who purchased the first book, "Its Called a Trout Stamp Not a Food Stamp," you gave me the spark to try to attempt another book.

Table of Contents

Prologue

I have lived a rather unique life. Being an employee in a mental hospital, serving in the Army, and being a police officer has left my mindset adjusted slightly from the norm. But my love for the outdoors has brought me into some great times with friends. However, not everyone understands my wit and personality. The stresses of my workdays have been relieved by hunting, fishing and friendships. Here are a few of those stories. They might make you scratch your head and wonder how in the hell I am still alive. Not just from escaping accidents but from my buddies not killing me due to my pranks and mishaps. I hope you enjoy. Pardon the grammar as once again I have tried to make it sound like me speaking in person.

THE PIGGY IN ME

I was reluctant to write about anything to do with my law enforcement career. However, it's a big part of my life, so I figured what the hell. I have been chasing bad guys for about a decade and a half now and in that time I have learned that it's not what you see on TV. We all get into this career thinking it's going to be all lights and sirens and that we are going to change the world. Well there are lights and sirens, but not near as often as you would think. The job consists of mainly sitting, typing and dealing with some pretty messed up things that most people could never imagine.

As for the changing the world part, I would like to think that we make the world a better place. But in the almost fifteen years I have been doing this I am still dealing with the same folks I did back when I first started. So, it doesn't appear that it's changing much. I have learned that with this career you get very close to your partners. It's a brotherhood, I don't know how else to explain it. You get a love, a true caring and concern for your partners. After all, you will go through things with them that you will never face with anyone else, even your spouse. Think about it, how many times have you and your spouse had to fight tooth and nail to get someone on the ground? How many times have you and your spouse been shot at?

The list could go on and on.

I have also learned there are two kinds of cops. There are those who were picked on as children and now have a badge and a gun. These guys are the tough guys. Then there are the sincere good men and woman in uniform who really care about people and want to make a difference. But no matter how the cards may fall each person in a uniform has to deal with some pretty horrific things. The way we learn to cope makes lawmen kind of unusual characters.

Imagine sitting across from a baby rapist who is telling in vivid detail of horrid acts, while you have to be nice to get a confession. Knocking on a person's door that you have known for years to tell them their loved one has been killed. Maybe running into a riot to save a person's life scared as hell and realizing that you failed to save that person. Talking to little kids who have been abused and telling them everything is going to be ok, when deep down inside you don't know that it is. Fighting with all you have to get control of a suspect and getting your ass handed to you while waiting for your partner to show up, being glad that they did but thinking it took them forever to arrive. Losing a friend to a horrible crime and having to face their family wishing there was something you could do to comfort them, knowing there is not much comfort to be found. Holding a baby that has died in your arms, thanking God it's not your child, but feeling empty as you see the parents. Having to cut the rope off of a person's neck after they attempted suicide, as they are cussing you for stopping them and later face them in public as though nothing ever happened.

Dealing with those thoughts give you dreams, dreams that don't ever go away. These thoughts and feelings change you as a person forever in the way you think, act and present yourself. I once read that the average cop's body experiences so much adrenaline that if an ordinary person experienced that same amount their heart would explode. Think about it, a normal day at work for us includes walking up to a car in the dark with no idea what that person is capable of. We have to consider that the baddest son of a bitch alive is driving that car until we can prove different.

It hits me kind of funny to think of all of the crazy bad things that we deal with but for the most part we do nothing. So it goes to show that we get paid for what we may have to do, not what we actually do. It is well known that most cops don't make squat for wages. We do, however, have one of the highest bankruptcy rates and the highest suicide rates of any profession there is. When the going gets tough the tough get going, which brings up another fact of the job. Divorce, yep that's a really high average compared to most any other profession out there as well.

So in order to cope with all the negatives, we officers have to adjust. We change ourselves in order to adapt. We accept the things that most people consider to be nightmares, to be our ordinary way of life. This adaptation happens with out us really knowing it.

I remember a class one time that I went to. The class was a sex crime investigation class. The teacher at the beginning explained to us that everything is not what it seems. At this point he tossed a softball to one of the students in the class. He told the student to toss it to another student, and to continue to pass the ball around until each student had caught it. This was to help us all get stretched out and relaxed. After the very last student caught the ball, low and behold if the instructor didn't show a nice picture on the screen. The picture of course showed the man's ass that the softball had been taken out of.

I tell that story to explain the mindset of a veteran officer. Things are never what they appear and if things are what they appear, they will most likely change. Officers like to help things change sometimes too. Above all, cops love to screw with each other.

This one time I had just witnessed a horrible event, a tragic moment for a family that was near and dear to my heart. It killed me to observe a family I was close to, go through that horrible loss of a loved one. I was taking it pretty hard and was about to break down in tears. I had no words to say, and everything I said seemed to make things worse. I went back to the station to fill out the paperwork and barely made it through the report. I was going home but didn't want to. I knew I would relive the event in my mind all night. I was having a 'feel sorry for me moment' and was not even the one who had to deal with the loss. I finally get everything done and call out to dispatch that I am going home. When I start my car to leave the station Holy Shit happens! I can't see a damn thing. The entire inside of my car is a cloud of white smoke, my car stereo is blasting as loud as can be, my siren is going off and my hazard lights are flashing. When the white smoke clears I can see that my light bar is whipping around and that my windshield wipers are on too. I am trying to shut everything off and see in the mirror that I now look like Casper the ghost.

I am laughing my ass off realizing that my partner had seen that I was upset and had broke into my car. He filled my defroster vents with baby powder and turned it on high along with every other switch inside my patrol unit. So when I turned on my key switch everything inside would go bat shit crazy. With everything going off at once it took me a second to realize what had happened. Which gave time for all of the powder to blow out all over everything. But the tragic event from earlier was the last thing on my mind for a while. Most people would think that was horrible timing, but something so crazy is really all that could make your mind break free. It kept me from having to go home right away. Hell I couldn't. It took me an hour to get my car vacuumed out. All the while I am standing around looking like the marshmallow man completely covered in baby powder. I had that shit all over everything I owned. I had the freshest smelling car and the cleanest pistol in the world for quite some time.

It got me agitated, but I had to laugh about it. There is this one thing about me, 'don't start none, there won't be none.' That is a motto that I have lived by, and continue to live by, in my day to day career. I too have pulled some shit with my fellow officers, as much shit as a guy can pull without going to jail anyway. Heck a time or two I probably should have been cuffed up.

My favorite story was with a guy who hated cemeteries. We would go patrol the cemetery at night and he would get all scared and lock the doors... as if doors could stop ghosts.

During his training we would go out there and I would screw with him. I would tell him how the spirits could be seen and heard by animals. I had him believing me and he was scared shitless about it. The next week I got a trap with a cat in it from animal control. I took it along with us during our nightly patrol of the cemetery. I told him how cats would go crazy if they saw spirits and he was going right along with it. So we get to the cemetery and let the cat out of the cage. It takes off as fast as possible and runs away. I am telling my partner how the cat must have seen a spirit. Knowing of course the cat just wanted the hell out of the cage, but it worked anyway. My partner was now even more scared of the cemetery.

'Patience and a good memory,' was a quote I was told early on in my career. Let me tell you it has proved to be the most truthful phrase I ever heard. After my partner had been screwing with me for a while, I remembered that cemetery event and thought, here is an opportunity. So I gather up about forty of the kids in town and promise them they won't get in trouble for helping me. We all paint our faces with the fluid from the inside of glow sticks and go hide out by grave stones around the cemetery. Then a random bogus call gets made to dispatch. So my partner, who I know hates the cemetery, is responding by himself to a suspicious person calling from the cemetery.

It is a full moon that evening and it is really cloudy. It is just spooky looking. As he is pulling in we all sit up and begin to chant. It looks like the cemetery has woken up and it sounds like the beginning of some satanic ritual. All the faces are glowing from the moonlight as we rise up from the gravesites. I see my partners face as he pulls in and I promise this is the closest he has

ever got to shitting his pants in his life.   He
approaches and we continue to chant. I have my
hand held radio so I can hear all the radio traffic.
He is calling for backup and it dawns on me that
I have just crossed the line. So I am trying to let
him know it's me out there in hopes to keep my
ass from getting in trouble. Now remember, I am
laying on the ground in all camouflage with a
glowing face and a radio in my hand. I try to
move so he can see me when he pulls out his
pistol and points it at me. Then he orders me to
show him my hands.

Laying there face down on the ground, I
begin to try to move my arms so he can see my
hands. As I move my arms, as he just ordered
me to do, he yells out at me again, "Don't move
or I'll shoot." So I am lying on the ground
thinking to myself, holy shit I have screwed the
pooch. This goes on for about three or four
minutes but he soon realizes it is me. However,
he still didn't put his pistol up.

My partner was not happy with me one bit.
He kept the pistol pointed at me the whole time
until I told him to put his gun up. All the kids
came up to him laughing and thinking it was all
funny, but he threatened to put all of us in jail.
So I am sweet talking him trying to make light of
things. It didn't do anything but make it worse.
He eventually left and we all went home and it
was a good two weeks before he would ever talk
to me again.

This behavior would most likely be unacceptable by most any other group of people but us cops. This is simply how we react and deal with some of the nonsense of the world.

There was another time where I responded to a suicide. It was a bad one. Blood, brain and guts were everywhere. The smell of brains is something you will never forget once you have smelled them. I am about to throw up and not wanting to be anywhere near this mess. I work it for quite some time and get the body released to the medical examiner. I have blood and guts all over me, I am sick to my stomach and have this horrible image in my mind that even writing this story has brought it back.

I go to the office and a fellow officer is laughing at me. He and tells me how he had the luck of the draw not having to deal with that call. He then tells me that he hates suicide calls and he would rather take any call but a suicide.

So, in my shallow little mind, after all of his screwing with me, I have realized just how to get him back. Along with some help, of some people who will never be named, I gather up a mannequin and crawl up to the rooftop of an old building. I call in a suicide call and here comes my fellow officer, who just thought it was funny as hell to screw with me earlier. He gets out of his patrol car and is looking around and calls out. "Is anyone here?" I scream back, "Yes, I'm here and I'm done with life." He looks towards my voice. It's very apparent he can't see me and doesn't realize he is being screwed with. He looks up towards the building and says, "Sir you need to calm down, it will all work out just fine." I play back and forth with him for a few minutes and he really is doing an outstanding job of negotiating with me. Right when he thinks he has this unknown person calmed down, I throw the mannequin off of the rooftop. He locks up and is looking straight up. He leans back watching the building and follows the body falling to the ground. The entire time his mouth is wide open with this 'Oh My God' look on his face. He is about to panic and cannot even talk. He just stands there, for what probably seemed like eternity for him, and in a split second he is cussing me and screaming my name. I guess when the mannequin hit the ground and the arm popped off he realized that he had been had. I am laughing so hard that I almost fall off of the building myself. It takes me a good ten minutes before I can even breathe.

I do have to say that I have had snakes, pepper spray and once even an armadillo inside my patrol car waiting for me at the end of the day. I have to admit I probably deserved it too. but it is what it is. We see and deal with stuff that there is just no normal way to cope with, and with that we turn to each other. There is not a cop in this nation that does not have some screwed up sense of humor and thinks, well let's just say, outside the box.

HOLY CRAP HOLY MATRIMONY

Have you ever thought you knew about a place or something, just to be shown you don't really know squat about it? Well this particular story has several twists about not knowing diddly shit about a place I thought I knew everything about. Me and Jenny are getting married and decide that a fly fishing trip is in store for a honeymoon. Now, I can't complain one bit about that. After all a fishing trip for a honeymoon has to be about as good as a guy could ever get. So to make the trip better for us, I decide that we will go to a place I am very familiar with, the coast of South Texas. Now, I have been here many times over the past few decades. I figured it would make it so much easier for us to do stuff, being I was so familiar with the place. I thought that with me knowing the area we could find stuff to do much easier and make it way more entertaining for the both of us.

So here is how it starts. After a long day of driving from South West Oklahoma to Port Isabel, Texas we get our motel room. We get unloaded and go to South Padre Island. My grandmother lived on the coast for several years and her ashes were scattered off the island when she passed. So it is a tradition to throw a dozen flowers out for grandma every time we go to the coast. So when we get to the island we go to the spot where grandma's ashes were scattered and throw the flowers. We ride around for a bit but go to the motel and try to get some rest. After all, we have been driving for quite some time and we are tired. The first thing on the agenda is a trip to Mexico in the morning.

So we get up in the morning and turn on our GPS. We soon realize that our GPS does not have Mexico. Now, Since I have been to Mexico a few times and vaguely remember what the area looked like where I had been before. So I decided we would just wing it. We head south to the Mexican border. I remember going to a Mexican town a few years back. It had a neat little shopping area and was just the taste of the Mexican culture that was rather neat to experience. As we are driving I am telling my wife, of one day, how neat the place is. That the signs in Texas will be in Spanish but when we get to the other side of the Rio Grande everything is in English. I tell her that the Mexicans are friendly to Americans and how much she will enjoy the culture.

So I see the sign that says International Bridge and off we go. We get to the first gate and speak with the U.S. Customs agent. He lets us through and we drive over the bridge. Now this is not looking the same as I remembered at all. But I tell Jenny that as soon as we get over the bridge there will be a parking area and we can get out and walk around. So we keep driving across the bridge and we get to the Mexican border agents. They are going through our stuff, treating us as if we have done something, and act very weird towards us. They get finished going through our stuff and give us the go ahead. At this point we head on south. I am looking for the parking area and it becomes apparent that there is not one. There is not anywhere to turn around and I begin to get a very uneasy feeling in my chest that I have gone over the wrong bridge.

We get into the city of Matamoras and I am looking for a place to turn around. Every time I try I get run off the road by a vehicle that doesn't understand what ALTO (the Spanish word for stop) means. The neighborhood is really rough. Each time we stop people are approaching our vehicle to wash the windows and there are hobos everywhere. We pass this really run down purple building that says DENTISTA on the front. There is trash and piles of debris all over in front of the dentist office. Everywhere we look there are homeless looking people and dogs running loose. There was a man in a wheel chair with no legs begging for money. I bet we saw at least three dogs loose on every city block. I am getting nervous and don't really know how the hell to get out of here and Jenny is not helping me much. Especially when she mentions that our truck insurance is no good in Mexico. We are both scared shitless. We end up turning thinking we could go around the block and get turned back around and get out of here. But that's not at all what happened. We turn and end up in this really bad neighborhood, I mean really bad. It's got to be the roughest place I have ever seen. Everything is trashy. All the windows are broken on the houses, it smells rotten and there is a big concrete block wall with razor wire on top of it all around the neighborhood, and again dogs running loose everywhere. I don't know how the hell to get out of the neighborhood so I turn on the first road I can. We end up in a neighborhood that is on the other side of the block wall. There is a big iron gate going into the neighborhood and it's apparent that these are probably the homes of the cartel. The houses are huge and really extravagant with Lincolns and Cadillacs in the driveway. As I am driving through trying to get out we see several peasant looking ladies walking in and out of the neighborhood. We assume they are servants at the houses. I do everything in my power to get out and on a road that looks familiar and the harder I try the worse I fail. And to make matters worse, I hear a DING DING DING, yep my low fuel light comes on. I forgot to get gas before we left. I didn't think we would be driving around so it didn't cross my mind. We continue to try and find a main road. The low fuel light dinging away making us feel more and more helpless as we try to get back to the U.S. And before you know it, the man with no legs in the wheel chair is on the road. So we turn towards him and get on track to get back in our country. Hell we even gave him money when we stopped, beings he was our saving grace we figured he should be rewarded. We finally, after what seems like an eternity but was actually only just a little more than a half hour, get back on the International Bridge North Bound to Estados Unidos. We are stopped in traffic but safely on the bridge. Everywhere we look there are Mexican men with machine guns staring at us. There was even a small size tank with machine guns ready to chase and kill. I am nervous as a whore in church and becoming more and more anxious to get over the damn bridge and the traffic is slow as hell.

We finally get to the U.S. side and the customs agent approaches our vehicle. Now keep in mind I have a huge metal tool box, the kind that require a forklift to pick up and are used on job sites, in the back of my truck that is full of our fishing gear. The agent comes up looking at the box, then looking at me and asks, "What's your business in Mexico?" I tell him we are on our honeymoon and wanted to see Mexico. He looks me in the eye with a really strange look, as if he thinks I am smuggling drugs across the border, and says, "This isn't a tourist town." It's not really looking promising for us to get home and he keeps eyeballing our big blue box in the back of the truck. He runs our passports and comes back. He now realizes we are scared shitless and really did got lost. He tells us this is a really bad place. That there have been several shootings lately and to get out of there and don't get out of the truck. He never searched our truck or the box.   He then tells us how to get to the part of Mexico I remembered going to and sends us on our way. As we wait for the light to turn green to let us through Jenny looks at me as serious as she could and says, "God doesn't rest until you go to sleep."

No matter how detailed the story or good the picture, going to that part of Mexico is an eye opener. You cannot imagine how helpless it felt unless you have been there. There are truly major problems going on down there and I thank God that we made it out and made it home to the U.S.

The next morning we planned on going fishing but mother nature had decided something else. So we decided to test our luck and try the other town in Mexico. We were both nervous but thought it would be neat to see it. We get directions to the Mexican town of Progresso. We head there and the sign says the same thing as the last one, International Bridge, so I didn't feel quite as stupid. It was just as I remembered. We found a place to park and walked across the river to a town that was very American friendly. We walked around and like

I told her most all the signs were in English. It was so Americanized that I asked for Pesos to bring back for the kids and they didn't even have any.

The clerk at the store had to go get some of his personal Mexican money because the registers were all full of American currency. Either way, we had a good time. We loaded up on candy, T Shirts and all the other crap that you don't need but have to buy when you go to Mexico. We head back to Port Isabel to go on a boat ride and see all the touristy things. Then we head in early for a fly fishing trip we have been longing for.

The next morning our guide, who has been highly recommended to us, cancels on us and it's just not looking promising. He tells us of a different guide and explains that he would take us. Now I am kinda pissy and not wanting a different guide, but it is what it is so we make the best of it. When we show up the guide is arriving at the dock about the same time as we are. He is super friendly and once on the water I decide that I am glad he is our guide. It kind of worked out better, our personalities meshed great and this guy knew fish. We were fishing for Reds in Laguna Madre, the bay between South Padre and Port Isabel. Now I have been to this place numerous times but had never fished the bay. As we are boating across the bay I realize it is nothing at all what I had thought it to be. On the way dolphins were even jumping up out of the water. I thought to myself, if your fishing day starts with dolphins swimming by it has up be a good day on the water.

The windstorm that blew through the day before made the water murky but it cleared up midday and was crystal clear. Our guide had a skiff boat and would push us from place to place with a large skiff stick to get us on the Reds. It was pretty amazing to watch these incredible fish as they would rise up and feed. They would 'tail' is what the guide called it. This basically means that as they feed their tail fin would rise above the water and you could see the spots on the tail. It was rather exciting to watch. It kind of reminded me of a shark fin coming out of the water.   As we are watching these fish rise and tail, the guide is explaining how the water is only about a foot deep in the whole bay. I cannot believe it! After all the years I had been coming to this place I never fished the bay because I couldn't get out in the water. Now I realize that it's a foot deep and I could walk most any place in the bay I would want to fish.

Our guide gets us across the bay to the coastal side of Texas and gets us right on the fish. This guy knew his business. He gets our rods and is showing us how to rig up. He realizes that I had put the fly line on my reel backwards. I am feeling like a complete fool at this point. I had my two year old daughter, Zoey, helping me with the rods and I screwed up and didn't get the line on right. I am thinking that this guy probably thinks I am a complete idiot. When we start fishing, he has me and Jenny rotate out casting his rod, due to me not knowing how to rig our own.

When my turn to cast comes around I get on the deck of the boat and go to make a cast. I cast forward, get my back cast and pull my arm forward to place my line and it goes all of about three feet. I am thinking to myself, what the hell just happened? I couldn't cast for shit, it was embarrassing.

First I cannot spool my reel right and now I am casting like I am some retard in the circus. So I get a tutorial on salt water fly casting. Now the guide is super nice and damn sure good at teaching.

So he gives me some pointers and before long I could get out a little ways, nothing compared to his perfect accuracy, but enough to suffice.

The first fish of the day comes up and the guide is telling me it is about five feet away. I am getting super excited and cast, and I am not even close. Yes, you read that right. It was five feet away and I couldn't get the fly on target. So after about five to seven casts I finally get the Red's attention and it takes the fly. It takes off and is gone, taking my fly line backing with it. I am so excited and about to pee myself. I am certain that I was screaming like a little girl but no one there would tell me I was. I get the fish hooked and the guide telling me what to do. I start to get the fish on reel and it's getting close to the boat. I tell the guide I want to keep the fish so I can get it mounted. The second I say that, the damn fish breaks my line and goes away. I feel like a complete jackass now. After all the work the guide did to get me on the fish, me not rigging my fly rod correctly and then my horrible casting problems, I break the fish off at the boat. The guide just looked at me and smiled and said. "Never talk about mounting or eating a fish that you haven't got in the boat." I took that to be some damn good advice

I gave the rod up to Jenny for a while and she got some pointers on casting and soon had it figured out and she go into a red pretty quickly. She casts right on the Red's nose and it takes her fly and runs. The same thing happens, she gets it to the boat and it breaks off. Now our guide is giving our no fishing asses hell. He rigs up a heavier leader and tells that this leader is made to catch the really big fish. He is doing it all in humor but I am reading between the lines. I need to listen to what this guy says. Because it's very obvious that I have no clue what the hell I am doing. So Jenny gets the new heavier line and begins to cast again. As she is mounting her back cast you can hear our guide make a loud noise. As I look back he has his hands on his throat, holding the line off of his neck. Jenny has cast and wrapped her line around the guide's neck, choking him as she brought her back cast forward. The guide got the line off and laughed but it scared the hell out of me so I can only imagine how he felt.

Jenny decided at that point to give the rod back to me. Our guide is poling us around and gets me on a group of Reds. He has some excitement in his voice as he tells me that one of the fish is a keeper. He points me to them and is giving me play by play of what it is I need to do. I cast, I miss. I recast, I miss. I do this about four times and finally the fly lands gracefully right in front of the Red. The guide tells me, "Wait, wait, wait, Ok strip the line." The very first strip I do, the fish just takes the bait. And holy shit wow, the line is gone! It takes all of about three seconds for the fish to take most all of the line I have on my reel and he is gone. I keep my rod tip up and reel him in, and then he takes some line back. This goes on for several minutes. My heart is pounding so damn hard that I can feel it. I have the shakes similar to that of a person whose sugar level is bottoming out. But I finally get the fish close and the guide helps me get the fish in the boat. I had just caught what was a pretty damn nice Red. It was nothing of a record but a damn fine trophy, suitable for anyone's wall. I was proud, maybe a little too proud. It was just minutes before that I couldn't cast for shit, didn't rig up my gear, pretty much just a dumb ass rookie at this whole thing and now I have landed a damn fine fish. I didn't say it on the boat or to the guide, but I will take luck over skill any day of the week. We continue to fish but we don't have much luck. The guide takes us all over the bay and I was completely amazed how the whole bay is less than knee deep. You could literally walk from the island to the bay. All these years, I could have been fly fishing in the bay and never realized how easy it would have been. The rest of the fishing trip was more of an educational trip and stopping so that me and Jenny could pee along the way. We had to stop so many times that the guide finally asked, "How do two people that have to pee so much meet? Did you meet each other on the way to the bathroom?"

At one pee break we had such an awkward moment that I thought I was going to fall in the water. I tell the guide that I need to go pretty bad and Jenny tells him she could go as well. She breaks out her 'Go Girl' pee funnel for women, which I got her for Christmas. The guide is getting as much distance between her and him as he can without falling out of the boat into the water.

Jenny is trying to figure out how to use the thing as the guide is so embarrassed that he has turned his head and is sitting on the back of the boat.

03.04.2012

As we are trying to finish out bathroom business Jenny just decides to step off the boat into about 12 inch deep water to pee. I am peeing off of the front of the boat. As Jenny is peeing I hear her fart, not once but twice. Now I am looking back at her as I am peeing and giving her a 'what the hell look.' She is so red in the face and I am trying not to laugh and make it worse.   I look at her and she has tears dripping down her face from laughing and is trying to stop her potty break as fast as she can. Now I am not talking about a little toot. No, she let out a manly fart and our pour guide was on the back of the boat not saying anything. But you know he was thinking to himself, what the hell kind of rednecks do I have on my boat. (I had to put that in the story. It's one of those things that will show proof if Jenny has read all the stories). As we get back in the boat and leave our awkward pee break the guide takes us around the bay. He gives us a lesson on all the different plants and fish that we came across.   It was a great experience. We even had a few stingray swim under the boat as we were out fishing. (Shannon did scream like a little girl when he attempted to touch the stingray, but he jerked his hand away instead. Just making sure you are reading babe).

We ended the fishing trip with a long ride back to the loading ramp. We bounced through the water at super high speeds, exactly opposite of the ride out. We get to the dock, unload our gear and go our separate ways. Hoping to come back and spend another day on the water with our newly made friend. And let me tell you this guy was awesome. He went above and beyond, even though Jenny tried to kill him and couldn't control her bodily functions in his presence.

We get the fish loaded up and I go to sit down in my truck. At this moment I realize I forgot something on the trip, sunscreen. I was sunburned so bad that I looked like a lobster. It got worse as the seconds went by. I could barely move my legs. The skin was so tight that I spent the next two days rubbing aloe all over them. I eventually peeled and looked like a snake for several days. But no matter how bad the burn, it was a great trip. Even Mexico was fun, well not at the time, but making it through such a crazy place was funny in its own kind of way.

I joke about the fear in Mexico but come to find out it really was bad. Numerous people during our trip explained several shootings and kidnappings that have happened over the few months before our trip. The State of Texas even had a warning for spring breakers to avoid Mexico because of all the crime with the cartel. It sure makes you appreciate being an American when you go and see first hand how bad other places can be.

This trip to the coast was a great one. We were married on the 29th of February and the first week of our married life was spent doing what we love to do. You know you have met your match and made your final catch when in the first week of your marriage, you experience such scary, funny, awkward and rewarding moments together.

IS IT BIGFOOT?

We all have places and spaces that are dear to our heart. I have one that has been pretty special for me as well. My step father raised me as his own. He worked all the time and we didn't do a whole lot of fishing or hunting, but when we did get a chance we always went to this spot. Well maybe not always, but more times than not this is where we went.

It is a river that forks into another river. I am not going to tell you where it is because I still fish there. I have learned that you never show a favorite fishing spot to another fisherman that you wouldn't trust with your wife. The place was rather scenic for out in the middle of farmland. There was an old railroad trestle that crossed over the river and every so often a train would pass. The banks were quite tall and hovered over the water fifteen feet or so and there were tall oak trees all around the banks. I first learned of this spot as a young child. We would dig worms and ride our bicycles to this place to catch fish. Growing up I didn't have a lot of friends, not because I stunk or anything, but I grew up in a really small town and there just were not many kids. The couple of us that did grow up together always went to the railroad trestle to fish. Every time I went it made me feel like a real life Tom Sawyer. I mean after all in this day and age you just don't see kids riding their bicycles home from the river, with a stringer of catfish hanging over their shoulder, a Folgers Coffee can of worms in one hand and a fishing pole in the other.

As I grew older and could drive I continued to fish this spot and would take a john boat with me. Me and my buddies would always spend the night, almost till morning, throwing fish in the boat. It was what we did. We were not the typical partying hell raising teenagers. Well I may have to retract the hell raising part, but we would much rather be at the river than most anywhere else.

Me and my dad would continue to go there as I got older. We would take a small john boat and slide it down the bank. We would go up and down the river tying 'limb lines' to the trees. A 'limb line' is just a line with a hook and sinker tied off, similar to a trot line. We would tie these to the trees, go down river to the next spot and repeat this over and over until we made it down one side of the river to the fork. We would then do the same thing on the way back. When we got back up to the spot where we started we would go check the lines. We would gather up our fish and reset the lines and repeat this process for several hours throughout the night. Usually by time we left we would have a cooler full of cat fish and a good time was had. Now my step dad, I won't use that name again as he was a dad to me, but for sake of explaining who he is, I clarified it. My dad is a hard working, person and doesn't say much. But when he does it's always worth listening to. The man never cussed, right opposite of myself.

Me and dad would go there a couple times a year and just enjoy a night on the river catching fish and more important, catching up. We would shoot the bull and have some quality time that work tried to keep from us. We did this a lot, and as I grew older and became an adult I enjoyed it more and more. Before long we gained another fishing partner. My uncle Joe had moved into town and he would go with us.

Now if me and uncle Joe ever did anything it was worthy of talking about. We had a black cloud that followed us on most all of our, let's just say, adventures. One time while out at the trestle on one of our adventures me, dad and uncle Joe are all in the boat. Keep in mind that my dad and Uncle Joe are not little people. They both are some pretty good size men. So when you put them two plus me in a ten foot john boat it doesn't leave much of the boat sticking out of the water.

Now my dad is a very serious person and me and uncle Joe are not by any means serious about much of anything. And when you get the two of us together it's like we actually get worse. We had been fishing all night and we would rock the boat back and forth on the water screwing with my dad throughout the whole trip. Now again, he doesn't say much, but as we go to land the boat on the bank, my dad looks at both of us with this serious grin, if there is such a thing. He is illuminated by very little moonlight and a dim lantern and states, "I know two boys who are going to get an ass whooping if they get me wet." Hell I was laughing so hard I could hardly function as he said it. Like I said before, he never says much and when he does it's worth listening to. Anyway we didn't get dad wet so made it out. Several years pass before I get to go back to that place for any kind of fishing. But one day, out of the blue, me and uncle Joe decide to go back to the trestle. Now before I go on with this part of the story I feel I owe you a better description of my uncle Joe. Uncle Joe is a big guy, about 280 or so and has a heart about the same. He is as good a man as you would ever meet in your life. He grew up in Eastern Oklahoma in the hills. He loves humor and will stretch a plan or a mission to the limit. He can do more with less and just has one hell of a time with most anything he does. He is as country as corn flakes and has no problem kidding around about being a hillbilly. Now Joe does know what a tooth brush is and I joke about him being a hillbilly but he is not like some character in "Deliverance." He is just a life loving country boy from the hills of eastern Oklahoma. A place where the men are men and the sheep are nervous.

I can remember one fishing trip that we went on and we were in my truck that I had just purchased. We are going to a river to fish and it's pretty muddy. There is a large puddle of water that we are driving into and as I get closer to the puddle I don't know that I can make it through. So Joe is screaming, "go go go" and I am thinking to myself, "stop stop stop." While hearing "go go go" and thinking "stop stop stop" I did a little of both. I continued to go through the puddle giving the truck as much gas as possible. Now it's dark outside so you cannot really tell how far the puddle goes. Once we were in the puddle you could damn sure figure out that the puddle was actually the river over flowing. So here we are in the middle of the water, giving the truck as much gas as possible and about to drive the damn thing straight into the river. Thank God I was thinking to myself "Stop stop stop." But either way we drove into enough water that we were not getting out of the mud. We were stuck. We are at least twenty miles from anything, it's dark, we have no phone, and we are stuck. So we take off walking down the highway to town. Once on the highway we are hearing noises of all sorts. Howling, yelping, and every other type of animal noise you can think of. I am nervous and realizing that Joe is too. He was always this big bad ass guy so I never would have thought of him to be nervous. But we are feeding off of each other's fear and before long we think we are being followed. So we are walking as fast as we can. It's about two in the morning and we have walked a good six to seven miles when a pick up pulls up. We finally get the break we need. As this pick up pulls up this good looking blonde asks if we need a ride. I am thinking to myself, I need your number and a ride. But right now a ride was way more important.

So I get in the front and Joe gets in the back of the truck. This gal was pretty damn hot, somewhere in the area of donut grease. So I am using my A game trying to impress her. The more I am talking to her the more I can smell the odor of alcohol. It's about two in the morning and it's starting to make sense. She has just left the bar and was driving home drunk, and while trying to impress her I told her I was a police officer.

Well let me tell you something, telling a drunk driver that you're a police officer doesn't really impress them at all. Basically it gets you dropped off. So now here we are dropped off. We find our way to a police station where we call my parents. I know, I know. I am an adult stuck in the river and had to call my mommy, but that's just what I did. So we waited for them to come pull us out of the river and take us home.

There was another fishing trip where we were crappie fishing at the same river where we had gotten stuck. We are moving down the river and above Joe I observe a nest of snakes. Now there is nothing in the world that scares me more than snakes. If something can move faster than me and has no feet, that just makes it plain scary. The nest looks like a big green ball of slimy spaghetti moving around in a bush. Well that scares me a whole bunch, enough to even make me pee a little.

We continue down the river, right towards the snakes. I get so damned scared that I can't think to talk or do anything else logical. Joe has his back to the tree so he doesn't even realize there are any snakes. I couldn't talk but I could, however, get right up to the snakes, scream like a little girl and jump out of a perfectly good floating boat right into the river. Leaving my uncle in the boat that almost flipped over as I went running across the water. Now I am not comparing myself to Jesus, but I am pretty sure that I walked on water that day. I know I made it to shore so fast that I didn't get very wet at all. When I got to shore I realized that I about flipped Joe out of the boat. The snakes got scared and were falling out of the tree right into the water I was running through, as well as around and in the boat that Joe was trying not to capsize. So let's jump back to the story of the trestle. Now I have learned that Joe gets a little spooked by noises in the night and if me and him are together, if it can go wrong it will go wrong. So here we go, we get the john boat loaded in the truck, yep the same truck we tried to drive into the river. Now my wife, his wife and even my parents are reading us the right act before we leave as if something was about to happen. We get our gear loaded up and we head to the trestle. Once there, we load up the boat with the gear and push it into the water.

We get on the water and it's just a weird evening. The clouds are covering the moon like some kind of scary Halloween movie. It's quiet, scary quiet. All you can hear is splashing up and down the river where fish are jumping. You cannot see very far in front of you and the lantern isn't doing much good. The best I can recall we lost a mantle on the lantern. We are setting lines and moving the boat down the river. As we are letting the current take us down the river, the battery on the trolling motor is starting to die off. So going up river, fighting the current is becoming a pretty tough and very slow process. We're about a mile from where we parked, it's still very quiet, and you only hear a splash here and there. A group of coyotes are howling down river a bit and we are just inching down the river trying to get back. You cannot hear any traffic and the fish have even started to slow down on the splashing. So it's damn quiet, and damn quiet gets damn creepy really fast. I am oaring along with the motor but the current is pretty much kicking our ass. After about thirty minutes we have gone probably twenty feet. I get close to the bank and try to start pushing ourselves back.

As I am pushing, Joe gets this startled look on his face and whispers to me, "Did you hear that?" And I whisper back, "Yes I did." You can hear foot steps walking by us on the bank. Not like a dog or cat foot steps, like something big. We are trying to make the boat go faster and it seems like the more panicked we got the slower the boat went and the closer the foot steps got.

The footsteps were loud, you could actually hear the branches and leaves cracking under whatever it was as it stepped. Joe is looking at me and telling me let's get out of here. And I am thinking to myself, that's been my plan for the last twenty minutes, but I can't get this damn boat to move any faster. As I am thinking that to myself I see a set of eyes. The eyes are not close to the ground and they are glowing green in color. I look at Joe and before I can talk he, in a holy shit scared kind of voice, says, "Yes I see them." I have the oar in my hand and cannot move this boat against the current any faster. We see the eyes, hear the footsteps and a moaning kind of grunt every so often. This goes on for a good hour as we are trying to get the hell out of the water. The faster we go the faster the footsteps go following us all the way to where we parked. We could never see what it was, just the glowing green looking eyes. But

each time it took a step it seemed louder and
louder.

We get to the truck but I cannot get the boat
up the bank. The noise is closer than before. It's
right across the river from where we are
standing, and the more I struggle the louder the
grunting sound gets. It takes me a few minutes
to get the boat in the truck. During the struggle
me and Joe both brought up the idea of just
leaving the boat in the river.

We get the boat in the truck. Then we hear a
splash of something in the river in the direction
of the noises. I get my light and shine over to
where the noise is coming from but I can't see
anything. My light is about burned out and
doesn't have much of a light at all. I am not
spending any more time looking around for
anything but my keys, to get the hell out of here.
We finally get in the truck, forgetting half of our
stuff and start to head out of there. Along the
way I ask Joe what he thought it was and he
looks me square in the eyes and says, "Is it
bigfoot?" Now I don't know if he was screwing
with me at this point but he is serious as a heart
attack when he asks me. So I go along with the
story and we talk about big foot. He goes on to
tell me how they have them in eastern
Oklahoma. I am thinking to myself, just how
full of shit can a guy be, but he was serious and
you could tell he believed what he was saying.

A couple of days later I went back to the

trestle during the day. I saw where there was a camper parked and the remnants of a meth lab. It was near where we were fishing and you could tell that people had been in and out of that area for that crap. I never went back to the place after that but we have brought it up in conversation over and over. Joe to this day thinks it was a big foot and I just haven't had the heart to tell him any different.

WHAT ARE YOU DOING THROWUP?

I am not really scared of a whole lot of anything. There are just a few things I am scared of and they kind of make me want to pee myself. Those few things are: snakes, that has to be the worst for me, midgets and flying. I hate to be scared of anything and I try to face those fears to overcome them when they happen. I have never been able to get over the fear of midgets or snakes. Now I know that sounds funny, but midgets are something you just don't see in my neck of the woods. They are not really scary but they do kind of make things awkward, but I am ok with that. Snakes on the other hand, scare the willies out of me. I have been told on countless occasions, by my friends, that snakes are not going to hurt you and most are not even poisonous. They may be right, but it's not their poison that has me concerned. It is my heart saying 'screw this' and giving out on me when I go into a panic attack, running and screaming like a little girl with pee dripping down my pant leg when I see one. So I have just said to hell with even trying to overcome that fear. After all, anything that has no legs and can move faster than me has the right to have me scared. But flying, I think, really what's the problem with flying? I can beat this fear.

It all starts in the beginning of my law enforcement career. I have met a couple of young guys who are pilots and are pretty damn good. They had offered for me to go flying with them on a couple occasions and I thought, no I am not going in the plane. I am not worried about the flying part, it's the sudden stop when you crash that I am worried about. Now I have a pretty strange sense of humor and tend to screw with people a little more than I ought to. I guess I did that to these pilots a bit when they were growing up. They remembered that great lesson in life I mentioned earlier about patience and a good memory.

So they finally talk me into a flight and I am nervous. I am not wanting to show it for the fear of them making fun of me but there is no hiding how scared I am at this point. I am so worried of crashing that I had nightmares the day before. But I figure if I ever want to get over this fear I have to man up and do this.

It's a hot summer day and I have never been on a plane before in my life. So getting in a little four seater plane isn't really helping me much at all. I get in the back and I am looking at the plane. I see how it is just a real small tube frame with super thin metal on the outside. There is not enough metal to protect crap if this thing decides to not make it. I have the shakes and we have not even left the runway yet. Hell we haven't even gone five feet. I am sitting in the rear seat and I have hold of the front seat so hard that my knuckles are turning white. I can hardly breathe. My buddies are laughing at me and cannot even closely imagine how nervous I am.

We take off from the runway and we get in the air. It's not as bad as I figured it would be. It's a different feeling and I am calming down a bit. When I say a bit, you need to understand that I am nowhere near calm, just not on the verge of having a seizure.

We are flying around and they are showing me the aerial view of several places where I grew. I was fascinated with how different things looked from above. We covered a lot of area. I got to see my house and several places where I hunt and fish and I became very fascinated. I was thinking how many new places I had just seen in such a short time and how I could find new areas to hunt, fish or find bad guys if I could fly.

We continue to fly around when they realize I have calmed down and that was not a good thing in their eyes. So they take me straight up until the plane stalls, then we go straight back down with no engine running until we almost hit the ground. Then the engine starts back up and we fly off and go around again. Now, my stomach has never really experienced my lunch going from the bottom to the top and back down. I can feel my stomach bubbling and I am not sure if I am about to throw up or shit myself. Either one could end up happening. Considering we are inside a small little plane up in the air on a hot summer day, neither can be good.

My buddies all realize I am nervous so they fly me around real calm for a little bit and I settle back down. I lose the fear of crapping all over in the air and making a genuine fool of myself. I mean after all, it doesn't matter what you do in life, but if you shit your pants while flying with your buddies, that's what people are going to remember you for.

But as things would have it the flight went well and we headed back to the runway. I had calmed down and was really enjoying the experience. We pass over the runway to make sure it is clear and we begin to approach for landing. Now this is where it gets funny. As we come in for landing I begin to squeeze the seat in front of me again. Like I said earlier, I am not scared so much of flying, it's crashing back into planet earth that scares the hell out of me. As we are coming in no one in the plane is talking. There is no noise whatsoever and everyone has this really serious look on their face. Out of nowhere this really loud buzzing noise starts. Then this other noise starts beeping loud. I am grabbing the seat in front of me and everyone is quiet. This noise continues to go BEEP, BEEP, BEEP. I am trying to figure out how to jump out of the plane that is still not on the ground.

Everyone inside the plane begins laughing but me. I cannot laugh for the fear if I tried my bladder would let loose everything I had been holding back for the last few minutes. I am not sure what just happened but I do know that I got a little bit closer to Jesus over those few seconds.

We start to land but the beeping and buzzing noises continue until we were on the ground. When we landed, they explained to me that it was just the stall warning on the plane. It is a sensor that lets you know when you are at a slower speed or something similar. So they had this all planned to pay me back for screwing with them. And boy did it ever work. I am pretty sure that ten years were taken off of my life that day. But I made it on the ground and thought it was great. I thought it was so great that I talked them into teaching me to fly. I figure that if you are gonna do something, do it big, right?

So they decide that it would be fun for me to learn to fly. After all, one of them is a pilot instructor. So we get things started. I would go to the airport and would take lessons for a few weeks learning various things about flying. I was as proud as anything I had ever done when I got to watch my instructor put the first entry in my pilot log. I felt like I was king crap for a while. I would read and read and pretty much all I did was research flying.

The lessons started out pretty easy. We would do touch and goes to learn to land and take off. We would learn how to get out of a stall, along with keeping speed and altitude and other things like that. It became really fun, but my instructor made me nervous. It was not his fault at all for making me nervous. It was one of those things where I had done just a bit too much research and learned just how good he was. I also learned he was just a tad bit crazy. He was a crop duster pilot.

During my readings I learned that there are a few crazy people in this world. You don't really have to talk to them to figure it out. Just by doing what they do for a living can convince you of it. Think about it, bomb technicians, alligator hunters, tight rope walkers and crop dusters are all just spun a bit different. I read where the average life expectancy is in the mid-thirties for a crop duster. They have to fly close to the ground, under power lines, dodge animals, trees, tractors and everything else you could imagine. The men have nerves of steel.

So we go for a few lessons and I am getting more and more comfortable but the lessons are getting harder. We get to the point where we are flying around an object. While flying around the object, we are keeping speed, elevation, and distance from the point. My instructor is telling me to fly the plane, don't let the plane fly me. He says to me several times to think ahead of the plane and the plane will respond to your actions. He stressed how you don't want to have to react to the plane or it's too late. You should always be ahead of the game. I keep thinking, hell I don't know if I am smart enough to fly. I am getting nervous and am not really feeling well. I had not eaten that day except for a pop and a candy bar. My stomach is growling and I don't know if it's hunger or nerves.

I get the plane up and have made several circles around our target point. My buddies are up flying around me and my instructor, watching us. It was pretty cool to look out and see the other plane but somehow that made me even more nervous. It was as if more pressure was added. I didn't want to look like a fool to my buddies. Worrying about not looking like a fool made me do just right opposite of that.

We have made a couple of passes and are on the third pass. I am supposed to be banked around a thirty degree angle to keep my elevation off the ground. There were cattle in the field under us. I was looking at them and noticed that they were getting larger each time I looked at them. I looked at my instructor hoping he would tell me what to do, and got nothing. So I keep flying and before long the cows are life size and I am about to stroke out. My instructor just sits there as calm as can be. I am about to make myself, my instructor and his plane fertilizer by crashing in the field if he doesn't help and he is calm as can be. I am so damn scared that I am about to cry. This goes on for what feels like days but I have no clue how long it really was, a few seconds I would guess. Finally my instructor looks at me with a smile as calm as can be and says, "Want me to show you how to get out of this?" I am thinking to myself, Really? You had to ask that question? The only reason you wouldn't want you to take over is if you wanted to meet Jesus in just a few seconds. At this point he does some kind of loop to get us out of this mess. I have no clue what the hell just happened but I do know that everything that was inside my stomach has now moved towards the top of my throat.

I am looking at my instructor and I can feel that I am about to throw up all over the plane. He is scrambling to find me a puke bag. Now I am also starting to realize that if you fart around this man he is going to puke himself. So when he realizes what is about to take place there is some panic in his face too. Now it's nice to realize a person is human and has fear, but it was better knowing he had nerves of steel. I now have both hands holding pressure over my mouth and I am getting hot, really hot. There are beads of sweat dripping off of my head, and my instructor is looking at me with a very unsettling look. I continue to holding as much pressure as I can over my mouth.

This is where it gets bad. Some things in life you have to be there to understand. I will do my best but I don't know how a person could explain this moment of my life on paper. So here we are, my instructor is in the beginning stages of panic mode, my buddies are flying around us watching me completely screw up everything I had been taught, and I am holding major pressure on my mouth trying to keep yesterday's lunch in my mouth until we can get on the runway.   But as things usually go, I fail. Before I can do anything the major pressure I was holding was not major enough. In between my fingers vomit begins to seep. OK maybe not seep, it comes shooting out and going all over the place.   I am dizzy and this is the worst smelling vomit ever. It is dripping off of the interior roof of the plane and landing in the hair and on the clothing of both me and my instructor. I cannot see, I am hurting bad and the smell of the vomit is so bad that it is making me even more sick. And did I mention, it's making my instructor sick too. He is trying to fly, trying to breathe and in the back of his mind is thinking of a place to hide my body after he gets me on the ground and kills me for puking on him.

He gets the storm window on the plane open and he is sticking his face out, trying to breathe. He is making a B line to the runway trying to land the plane. I am feeling about as stupid as I ever have. I am looking at my instructor and he is looking at me trying not to throw up.   The instrument panels are covered in this very thin soda colored liquid that just came shooting out of the bottom of my stomach and it just keeps on coming. I cannot see anything other than puke dripping off the ceiling of the plane and landing all over both of us.

We get to the runway and begin to land, we skipped doing a passover and just went straight down on the runway. I cannot see much and damn sure have no clue what is going on. As we are landing I hear a very loud noise and all I can see, through the vomit covered window, is the bottom of another plane that is directly on top of us. Like right on top, inches away from us. We get the plane on the runway and stop it in record time. Both of us bail out. I am still puking and now my instructor is gagging. I don't know that he ever vomited but he sure got close to it. I am on the ground covered in puke. We are taking off what clothing we can without getting too personal out there.   As we are trying to decontaminate ourselves my buddies come in for landing.

When my buddies get landed one of them had a look in his eyes like he just met Jesus and the other is looking in confusion wondering what the hell just happened. I am still throwing up all over and feel like I am about to die. When I look in the cockpit of the plane and realize the mess I am going to have to clean up I definitely wanted to die. But they all begin to laugh when they realize what happened. The one who looked like he met Jesus got to see the top of our plane up close and personal. The other told me that he thought I was flying really good and then didn't really know what the hell happened. He didn't realize all that swarming around was not intentional, that it was me trying to turn us into liquid people spread on a field in rural Oklahoma .

After we all settled down, somewhat cleaned up and everyone was done laughing at me I had the shittiest job I have ever had to this date. I cleaned all the vomit out of the plane. I say all, but I stand corrected, my buddies explained to me that there were still chunks that wouldn't come off. More than once they explained just how bad I made their plane stink. So I guess I didn't get all of it out. But that had to be the nastiest thing I have ever done.

I did go back in the air at a later date and went through some more instruction. To this day every time I see my instructor who was a good buddy of mine, he asks me, "What are you doing Throw Up?" We both laugh, but it has been over a decade and I still feel awful about it. But I guess sometimes in life you have to do things so people won't forget you.

TALK NASTY TURKEY

Well this all starts in a mental hospital about fifteen years ago. No, I was not a patient, I worked there. And yes, as everything else in life you become a product of your environment. I was in my early twenties and somewhat rough around the edges. This was my first 'real' job and it landed me a spot being a mental health worker. Now let me tell you I have done a lot of cool stuff in my life but working in a nut house had to be one of the most fun. You would see things there you couldn't imagine. Cable TV had a hard time topping every day at my work. I learned a lot about life working at the nut house. I had never really met any so called 'crazy' people in my life. But the longer I worked there the more I realized, hell I may be crazy.

I have been accused multiple times of escaping from that place as a patient not an employee. More important than realizing I may be crazy is that I met one hell of a lifetime friend working there.

Now this friend I met, I am not really sure how we became friends. Because when we first met he, Kenny, was my boss. And at this particular point in my life I was probably not the greatest employee. If he had an option I don't believe he would pick me as an employee. But either way a friendship was made between two guys and it has lasted a lifetime. That lifetime friendship probably had something to do with helping me grow up a bit and calm my crazy ass down.

We both worked nights and after the patients went to sleep we would hang out shooting the bull all night. Before you know it we both realized we had a common ground. We both had a passion for the outdoors. We spent countless hours discussing hunting and fishing trips that we had been on. We would talk about dreams of future hunts we wanting to go on and hoped to get a few of them together. We did get to go on one local fishing trip but that was all we got to do during that time in our lives. We would hang out sometimes after work and he soon introduced me to his family.

Now this part is pretty special to me. I met Pops, who just happened to be one of the most interesting people I have ever met in my life. The man had to be borderline genius. I mean this guy could make anything with almost nothing. I soon realized that me and Pops had a lot in common as well (not just both being borderline genius). We both shared a passion for fly tying. Fly tying is something I love to do and I did for several years as a child. After not tying for several years, Pops sparked that fire and got me back into fly tying.

Our friendship grew distant over the years with me choosing a new career and joining the Army. Every so often we would stumble back into each other and each time we would it was the same conversation about needing to get together and spend some time outdoors. It just seemed like we would never get to the great outdoors.

I stumbled into Kenny one day and he told me to come by and visit with him and Pops. Several years had gone by since I had talked to Pops or Kenny. I went by and we all sat and shot the bull together. They had started a new hobby. They had started to make handmade turkey calls. I was impressed with how they were all patterned similar but each call had its own personality, either by unique woods or by workmanship. I was pretty excited to own one of their calls. I ended up buying several calls from them that day but never got to hunt with any of them. I kept one and sent the others to buddies for gifts. All of us thought they were too pretty to use for hunting, so they all ended up displayed.

I ended up leaving that day quite impressed with how far along they had gotten with their young hobby. But knowing them, I was not surprised. They had always made things by hand. I can remember the first time I went to their shop. They were showing me long bows that they had made themselves that were as pretty and performed as good as any thing you could ever buy in a store.

Well, years went by again but not near as

many, and I stumble into Kenny again. I am at a local retail store and we come across each other. And you guessed it, we talked about getting together and doing some killing.

This time we did. We met up and decided to do some spring turkey hunting. Now I was super excited to go with these guys. Not just to spend time with a lifelong friend, but to see some of these calls in action. I had finally gotten past the part of thinking they were too pretty to hunt with and busted out some of the calls to see if they really work.

We met up to do some turkey hunting and headed to a remote part of Northwest Texas. We were laughing all the way to the field. Pop's sayings and catch phrases are enough to make anyone laugh till they pee on themselves.

We get to where we are going and after fifteen years me and Kenny are finally in the woods. We get set up in a ground blind and get things fired up. Kenny starts to purr on his slate and box call and the toms are all beginning to gobble. The turkeys respond to these calls in rapidly fast order. They are coming from all angles and I am so damn excited that I am getting the shakes. Kenny is explaining to me what the calls are supposed to sound like and begins to give me a lesson with the calls.

I bust out the calls that have just been desktop displays for the last few years and start to give it a whirl. Kenny is laughing at me as I attempt to use the call. I have never really used a slate call prior to this hunt. I am trying to not look like a complete dumb ass, but Kenny is having a hard time holding it in. As poorly as I am calling the birds are still coming in. I told Kenny that the toms probably think that my calling is some retarded hen running around out in the field. They are running in thinking that her being retarded would make it easy to get what they want from her.

At this point Kenny is laughing so hard that I don't know if we are going to recover but the turkeys are getting closer. We finally settle down and are getting ready to take our shot at this tom that is strutting closer and closer. We are archery hunting. Because if you are hunting with Kenny and Pops, that's how you hunt, because they only archery hunt. The turkey continues to get closer to archery range. All of the sudden some guy comes driving down the farm road with a loud pig trap trailer behind him and he scares off the toms. It's hotter than hell and the birds got spooked, so we decide that there is always another day.

We end up leaving the hunting spot and decide that we should go eat lunch before we call it a day. On the way to lunch I am asking Pops about calls and what each one means. They had a specific call pattern that they used at different times, so I was curious to what they represented. Pops showed me how a box call takes one long purr then four clucks when you are calling in toms. Then he says, "You won't ever forget it, if I tell you what it means." With as serious a look on his face as a man could have he got the call. He began to make the sound while saying, "I want some, dick dick dick dick." He then looks back to me and says, "that's what it means. That's what the hen is saying to call in the tom."

I am laughing so hard and everyone in the truck is laughing so hard that I have no idea how we didn't wreck. We end up leaving for lunch. Stories were told and good times were had at that lunch table. Some were so damn funny that you want to share them, but I am not sure that these stories were made for public reading.

We end the day with no such luck as far as turkey hunting. But it was one of the most successful hunts I had ever been on. It was fifteen years of hopes and dreams that finally came true. And to me, the time with friends in the outdoors is way more important than killing five thousand birds. Those are memories that nothing can ever replace.

We made plans for another hunt and actually get together again for another morning hunt. We get set up and again, stories were told along the way that will just make you cry from laughing so hard. As we get set up Kenny is making fun of me and telling me to do my retarded hen. He is even getting text messages from our buddy who was with us the last hunt, asking about the retarded hen call. As we are visiting, Kenny gets the turkeys gobbling in fast time again. We see a few toms at a distance and they are all coming our way. But out of the woods comes a big dark shadow instead of a turkey. At first me and Kenny both thought it was another hunter. But as we looked through our binoculars we could tell that it was a big wild pig. I learned that day that turkeys don't like pigs. As soon as the piggy came out the turkeys went back into hiding for a while. Before we could even get settled back in to call them, a large group of pigs comes strolling along across the field. There were probably twenty adults and several piglets. They come walking across the field and walk straight to our blind. As they are getting closer they observe our turkey decoy and act somewhat spooked by it. They start to walk off to the south of us. Kenny looks at me and says, "Let's get out and stalk one for a shot."

I am thinking to myself, 'Kenny your nuts, we only have bows and there are twenty big pigs and were gonna 'sneak' up on them.' So I tell him, "Sure let's try that." Now I have no intentions of getting remotely close to these pigs. I figure they will be so far gone by time we get there that we will never be able to get a shot on them. But I figure what the hell, if you never try something you will never be successful at something either.

We get out of the blind and I tag along behind Kenny. Now, he is a great hunter and I figure if he says it is possible then it must be. We sneak through the wooded area about fifty yards and right in front of us in a clearing are the pigs. As I am looking in awe that we had snuck up on them, Kenny pops off a shot and the pigs go ape shit nuts. They are running around in every direction. I am standing around wondering what the hell to do, wishing I had a gun of sorts to keep from being ate by pigs. As I am standing there I see a large sow. She is just standing there looking at me. She is in the wooded area about forty five yards out. I look and see it's a clear shot to her right through all the trees. So I pull my bow up, sight her in, and send an arrow down range.

Not to brag or anything, but it is my story after all, so I guess I can a little. This shot was farther than I had my sights set on my bow so I adjusted the best I knew how. I was surrounded by a bunch of pissed off pigs and standing in very thick brushy forest area. Everywhere you looked there were oak trees. There was not a tree that was more than two feet from another tree. So when I took the shot I figured I just donated an arrow to mother nature. But no, as I look up I hear a thud. The pig makes a move, unsteady on her feet. I stand there trying to catch my breath and cannot believe that I hit her.

I go to look for my arrow, considering I might have missed. Even though I knew that I had hit her, it was such a awkward shot I had some doubt in my mind.

When I get to where the pig was standing I do not see any blood, my arrow is not there and the pig has left. I am thinking I missed but cannot find the arrow, so I am not certain one way or the other. All of the sudden I see her standing against a tree and it looks like she is about to fall down. I stand back to let the arrow do its damage. I let the pig calm down so don't have to chase her for miles and miles. As I am looking at her, the forest is taken over by loud sounds of grunting pigs. They are in every direction and they are getting louder and louder. I whistle for Kenny but get no answer. I am thinking that I am about to get attacked by some Texas piggies and only have an arrow to protect me. I am confident with my bow but not even Robin Hood would have a chance if all of these pigs came at once. I continue to whistle for Kenny and nothing. So I begin to walk forward to see if I can find the pig.

I have it made up in my mind that I am going to get that pig. I know I have hit it and I also know that if I cannot find it Kenny will never believe that I have shot one. I walk for about a hundred and twenty yards through the brush. All of the sudden I hear the loudest squeal I have ever heard. I am thinking to myself 'oh shit' the pigs are coming and they are mad. But then it just gets quiet. I go to see what the noise was and all of a sudden Kenny pops up and tells me he just shot a pig.

I tell him that I did too but can't find it. He looks at me like I am full of crap. Now I realize I am full of crap but I wanted him to believe that I had killed a pig. So I go with him to see the pig. When we see it, I tell him that it's the same pig that I had shot just a few minutes earlier. He looks at me with this 'yeah right' look and we go approach the pig.

Kenny grabs the pig to drag it out and when he does, there is my arrow. Which means that we both shot the same pig. So we drag the pig back a couple hundred yards to where we were parked. We both decide that this should be put on the grill, so we gut the pig out. We of course take some pictures with the pig first. By the time we were finished it was time to call it a day. Neither one of us had the energy to go on much longer anyway.

As the season came to an end we did not kill any turkeys. But that is what makes the hunt even more surreal. After fifteen years of trying, we finally get a hunt. To make a successful hunt we had to change target animals, but in the end two lifetime friends killed the piggy together.

After one hell of a season and lots of great memories it was nice to finally have a picture for the wall. Two buddies, who after all these years, finally made it happen. It always amazes me how the outdoors can build friendships and memories that will carry forever and can be passed from generation to generation.

I know for certain that I will have a memory that will make me laugh out loud for the rest of my life. When I hear that long purr and four sharp clucks a hen makes when calling a tom, it will take me back to the story from Pops of what a hen is really saying.

EXOTIC HUNTING

I have loved hunting for a couple of decades now and have this passion of having trophies mounted of every species that I can. To me, trophies are memories that we can pass down to other generations. They are actual 'things' that people can touch and look at. Some people may never get the chance to see certain animals in their life if it weren't for these trophies. So I try to hunt as often as possible and try to attempt hunts with different creatures every chance I get. Not just to fill the walls of my 'I love me room' but to teach people the beauty of nature. To pass on traditions from one generation to the next.

My grandfather was a taxidermist and he had a whole museum of animals in North Dakota. I remember going there as a child and being in total amazement. He had all these strange animals that I didn't know even existed and he had them preserved for people to see. So I guess it is grandpa's fault for making me think I need to hunt every critter on the planet. And as ornery as grandpa was I kinda get to be that same way to my kiddos. After all, I have a room with over a hundred mounts of various creatures and I have two daughters. I bet they will have fun deciding what to do with all of daddy's crap from his 'I love me room' when I pass on. Well as obsessive as it sounds, I try to never turn down the chance to hunt or fish for something new. I don't care if I cannot get the critter mounted. Just a picture with some of the amazing creatures God has blessed this planet with is enough for me.

I remember one hunt that I went on, I will not go into much detail on the hunt, for one reason it was not worth talking about. I was all worked up and ready to kill an animal that not only was delicious to eat but also was an odd looking animal that would be a great trophy to hang on the wall. I was going after a black buck antelope. I didn't have the ability to go to another country to hunt this thing at the time but had heard of the exotic hunting lodges around America.

So I make plans and go on my first exotic hunt in Southern Texas. Now this was an awesome looking place. I am not going to mention the name because I would not recommend it to anyone and I don't want to bad mouth them either. They had great accommodations and did in fact have trophy animals. But, and I mean a big but, it was not the kind of hunting that I would recommend to anyone.

I get to this place after a long drive and am greeted by some super friendly folks. They are more than willing to do whatever they can to help me, and to receive a tip. They get me unloaded and set up in an awesome room. I felt like I was in some old hunting lodge from centuries past. They tell me about the 'realistic' stalking hunt that is about to take place in the morning. I am worked up thinking how awesome this is going to be and don't know that I got even one minute of sleep. I lay there dreaming of being on some African hunting safari and before you know it, hunting time had come.

I get woke up by a young guy who works on the ranch. He is telling me about the hunt and how close to a real safari hunt it is going to be. He tells me how spooky the animals are and to make certain that I remain still while hunting. He is giving me common sense advice but stressing the 'realistic' fact over and over and over. So at this point I am somewhat agitated with the guy. He is making me feel like I am walking around with my head in my ass. The more he talks the smaller his tip is getting. So to jump to the end of the day, his tip consisted of me telling him to shut the hell up.

But anyway back to 'the hunt.' We get out and are getting gear loaded up to go hunt the trophy animal from another land far away. As we are loading our gear I hear metal banging in the not too far distance. It is getting brighter but there is still not enough sunlight to really tell what is going on. When the metal banging stops I can hear a couple guys with very broken English, and truth be known it was more like Tex Mex mix, talking. I can hear them going "ya ya ya" as if they are shooing an animal through corrals. At this point I am pissed off at the guy who keeps talking about this realistic hunt and now I am hearing these noises. My curiosity is piqued so I begin to ask questions.

I ask Mr. Know It All if they are shooing the animal that I am fixing to shoot. He gets a blank stare on his face and begins to make up all kinds of stories about what they were doing. He would not tell me it wasn't my animal but he wasn't telling me it wasn't either. I was soon catching on to what was really happening.

I am not really into shooting birds off their perch or shooting penned up animals, so I am about to tell these guys to skip rocks. As I tell the kid that this is not the type of hunting I am supposed to be doing, he begins to explain that it's very realistic. The animal is 'open range' and that they have a sporting chance. So I decide against all better judgment to go ahead and try this style of hunting.

So right when you think it cannot get any worse, I get proven wrong once again. I get on the ground and get set up. Through my binoculars I can see this animal I am supposed to be hunting. I can also see the lots that they chased him out of and that the poor animal is penned up in an area smaller than forty acres. I decide to tell the guide that he can take his hunt and stick it in whatever orifice of his body he would like too. He is just the hired hand and he knows he is in deep shit if he goes back with me that unhappy. He is doing everything he can to make me stay and shoot this goat grazing in a pen. But no matter how hard he tried, I was done. He gets me gathered up and takes me back. The great hospitality of the lodge allowed them to offer me a free hunt next time I wanted one. So if you ever want to go shoot a goat off of his feeder I have a free meal ticket.

I get loaded up to leave and as I leave I look at the animal through my binoculars. I am a bit disappointed that I won't have a trophy of my own. The story of the hunt I am going home with is surely not anywhere close to the story I was hoping to be going home with. While looking through my binoculars at this creature, that was in fact a true beauty of nature, the two Mexican men I heard earlier had a can of grain. They were shaking it calling the creature back to his pen and the animal just ran back like a pet. I learned right then that I didn't need to be super sneaky in order to not scare the animal. I needed to be sneaky so the animal didn't run up to me to get fed. All I can say is wow! What some people will do to make a buck.

I make it back to Oklahoma. I am not remotely happy about donating my money to such an operation and coming home empty handed. I tell some of my friends and they all give me hell. But hunting at home was more enjoyable and at least I could sleep at night after

I went.

I learned to appreciate my back yard hunting areas and would try to make the best of all of them. Every time my buddies would call I would come running, waiting to see what we were going to do next. And with the buddies that I hang out with, you just never ever know what they are about to get you into.

I can remember one time the phone rings and my buddy is on the other line.

"Hey bud."

"Hey."

"Want to get a bird?"

"Sure."

"I'll be there in a few."

"Ok, I will get ready."

"Ok."

My buddy comes to pick me up and has this shit eating grin on his face. He tells me that I am about to be on a mission I won't soon forget. He won't tell me what but tells me that we are about to get a 'bird.' Now this buddy raises quail and pheasants so I am thinking I am about to help him catch some of his birds that have escaped or something. NOPE! Not at all what he had planned. I know this because when we should have turned right to go to his house, we turned left. And standing in the middle of the roadway about a mile down the road was in fact a 'bird.' This was definitely not a bird I was planning on catching today.

Right smack dab in the middle of the road was a damn emu. This emu is pacing from side to side. All of a sudden I feel like I am a character from a Swiss Family Robinson novel we all read as children. My bud drives up closer and we both get out to figure out what we need to do next. I am not sure that either one of us had a plan at all. Hell I had no idea what to do. It takes more than a couple of seconds to go from thinking about catching quail to catching emus.

Now I am wondering what the hell is an emu doing here and more than that, I am thinking what the hell are we going to do with it when we catch it? I am thinking already 'when' we catch, imagining it will not be much of anything at all to do. For those of you that don't know, an Emu is a very large bird similar to an ostrich. They have been raised on farms for awhile but most of the people who raised them have gotten out of the business for some reason or another. Some of the people who got out of the business just let the birds loose as feral animals. And feral emus are just way too much temptation for me and my buddy to handle.

Now I have no clue what we need an emu for. I did a lot of thinking and I am certain if we can catch this big bird we will surely be the only ones who have one. So we sit in the truck staring at this bird trying to get a battle plan together. We finally get what we think is a plan and we both get out of the truck. Now it is somewhat chilly so I have an old army field jacket on and some gloves. We approach the bird and it's not really acting nervous at all. Now if it could talk I am certain that he would say the right opposite about us. As we get closer the bird just wants to stare us down. He is not stupid though. He is looking at us like he knows we are a possible path to food. My buddy has a lariat rope and as we get right up on the bird the thing gets just as nervous as we are and decides to have an attitude. My buddy gets the rope over its neck and the fight is on. Now I would have loved to have been able to see this show from the sidelines and not be a part of it. I am certain that we looked like total jackasses out there but we were not giving up one bit.

We have this bird on the ground, a rope around its neck and it is smooth pissed off. It has not one thought in its simple little mind of us catching it. He soon begins to fight, pulling away from us and taking us by the rope wherever he is wanting to go. I was in total amazement of how much strength these creatures have in their legs.

Well we have the bird. He is somewhat dragging us in circles and we are making no progress whatsoever. So I get the idea to take my field jacket off and throw it over the bird's head. As I do the bird seems to calm down for a second.

We somehow conjure up a plan to get the bird in the back of my buddy's truck. Of course I get to be the jackass to ride in the back. We still don't have a real idea of the strength these creatures have, but one thing for certain is that we are soon about to. The bird is ok for a few minutes but that few minutes was not long enough. We are going down the road and the bird starts to move a bit. I grab the bird and hold the field jacket and try to keep the bird covered and held down. Well let me tell you something, nothing was going to hold this damn thing down. As I am squeezing this thing it just stands straight up in the back of the pickup truck. We are now going down the road and I am all of a sudden riding bareback on a pissed off emu's back. I am not certain how long it took my buddy to stop but it was way too damn long. He does get stopped and just as any good friend would do, he falls to the ground laughing at me looking like a rodeo clown riding on big bird. He finally gets up to help me as this bird is literally kicking the hell out of me. And let me tell you another thing. When an emu kicks you it is something that you will not soon forget. We get the bird calmed down and we get back on the road. We are on a country dirt road but we have to cross a highway to get to my buddies house. So here is where the fun begins for round two. We are stopped at the stop sign about to cross the highway and the damn thing all of a sudden decides to kick the shit out of me again. So instead of stopping, my buddy decides that driving faster to his house, that is less than a half a mile away, will be a better option for me at this time. So for a half a mile I am on a mobile rodeo ride of sorts but instead of a bull I am on a damn bird. As stupid as it sounds I think I would take a bull any day over a bird. I have never been kicked so hard in my life as I was that day. As we are pulling up in the driveway, I am still hanging on for dear life and this bird is bouncing me around from one side of the truck to the other. The bird is as scared as I am and is pissing and shitting all over the place. Yes, as much rolling around with this thing as I am doing I am beginning to wear a lot of the bird's leftovers. We finally get to the pen my buddy has ready and he puts the tailgate down. I jump out while my buddy is laughing so hard I think he is going to have a seizure. The bird then jumps out and runs right into the pen to the food.

That bird was calm as can be and didn't act one bit mean once it was in the pen. I sure as hell won't volunteer to go help my buddy catch any birds in the future though. Hell snipe hunting would be more rewarding.

I laugh every time I think about the two stories. One high class 'exotic' hunt that was not cheap and the other just a phone call from a friend. The truly exotic hunt that I will forever remember didn't cost anything except a little pride and I didn't even have to travel five miles. Makes me think of the old saying that the grass is only greener on the other side because it's growing over a shit tank.

RAMBLINGS OF THE MAN WHO KILLED 1000 DUCKS AND 20 FRIENDSHIPS

I love the outdoors and I try to spend every chance I get out there. I hunt and fish for almost everything there is a season for. Out of all the types of hunting and fishing there are two that trump all other. Duck hunting and fly fishing. Yes both are great sports of solitude and both require a lot of gadgets. Well they don't really require a lot of gadgets but if you want a hobby that has a lot of gadgets, that you can feel justified in purchasing, these two hobbies are for you.

I love hunting and love the outdoors but don't really like people. I have been in law enforcement so long that I really get tired of being around people. So when I have some off time I want to be by myself. Duck hunting and fly fishing make that a possible option. Now I am not saying that I don't like other outdoor adventures. Those two just take most of my time and effort. There is a reason for this of course, and you got it, I am about to tell you that reason.

Growing up in Southwest Oklahoma, everyone hunted. Most people around these parts were so involved in hunting that it consumed them. My family really wasn't. My dad worked all the time to keep us high maintenance kids stocked up in whatever we thought we couldn't live without. But the other people around us were so involved that they would buy hunting and fishing stuff even if they didn't have money to feed their family. I didn't really do a lot of hunting with my family. Most of my relatives that hunted died off before I was old enough to join them on any sort of adventure.

When I became a teenager, that began to change. All my high school buddies hunted and fished. And man did they ever. Now there are several things in life I tend to blow money on, but with these guys I couldn't keep up. They hunted and fished year round and everywhere. They were damn sure good at shooting most any animal you could dream of. Some from the bed of a moving pick up. I didn't really think much of it though. My mom was rather strict so I wasn't able to be a part of the mobile hunting club. Few and far between I did get to go on some trips.

The good thing about my buddies is they respected you. If you didn't want to be a part of something, they wouldn't do it around you. So for the most part I wasn't around a lot of the shenanigans. I did like to be outside though. I had the continued problem of either not wanting to do it the way they did, or I didn't have the money to go out with the big boys.

As I grew older I learned some things. First if you want to be a certain way, hang out with people who are that way already. So I did just that. I had friends who I truly respected and who shared the same ideas that I wanted to have. Some of the best friends I have are from this time in life. If you stay true to yourself and your beliefs good and long friendships will follow. However, with me it seems that after a few years of friendship I tend to step on toes. Maybe I am just a little too bullheaded or set in my ways. But either way, those who have become my friends have remained my friends.

My friends from back then always hunted and they would drag me along on hunts that I had not been on. I am sure that it was for pure entertainment because I didn't really know crap about the outdoors. I was destined to be a story in someone's mind before the hunt even started. I was that guy that could walk through an entire field and step in the only pile of poop around. But my buddies took me along anyway. Most times they got what they wanted, which was entertainment. In the first book there was the turkey hunt where I broke my leg, and there are many more. But no matter who or where the story took place there always was just that, a story. I took things way to serious and had the 'go big or go home' mentality.

Simple hunts, like dove, I still took to the extreme. I felt that if I missed a hunt I was always one behind. I remember one year it was opening week for dove and the birds were flying in mass numbers. I had decided that I was going the next day come hell or high water. The only problem was that I was in the Army National Guard and it was drill weekend. So I conjured up a story and had it all planned to call in sick. My buddies on the other hand had better plans for me.

It's about eight in the morning right before first formation for my unit. I decide to stop hunting and call my first sergeant and let him know I was sick. Right as I do all of my buddies, who have been sitting there silent since the sun come up, decide to take their guns and unload them all at the same time. So here I am on the phone with my first sergeant, trying to sound like I am deathly ill and cannot make drill. When all my jackass buddies are firing rounds in the air. That day they gained me a new name in the Army. My first sergeant said I must have had 'bird flu,' and that is what they called me. I got a taste of karma on that hunt as well. I sat down in some bullnettle. Bullnettle is some kind of toxic plant that will make you swell all up. It's like you went on a date with some nasty woman with crabs or scabies. I got that crap all over my legs. I itched and was swollen for days.

Taking risks and trying not to miss opportunities has given me some funny memories and also kept me in touch with some buddies I have had all of my life. Dove season is the first season of the year and I try not to miss it. I have hunted with the same group for at least

20 years and to this day we go shooting every dove season. Most every time they get some sort of laugh. I don't know how we have made it so long without killing each other but we have, and that is amazing all in its own.

There have been numerous hunts that I have tried and some with success. Believe it or not most of the hunts I have been on usually end well. It's the simple ones that usually go wrong.

I still have this scar above my eye. You know its funny, when that is how you begin the story. But I do. Me and my buddy were going to shoot some prairie dogs. It's long range shooting at its finest and there is a never ending supply of the varmints. I needed to go hunting pretty bad, but didn't know it. I was going through an ugly divorce, was pretty depressed and needed to get away. Something I have learned is that if you are depressed, killing stuff usually makes it better.

This day started off kinda bad for my buddy. He calls and is trying to get me out of the house. I am giving him my pitty party story about how bad life is. He is tired of hearing about it and comes to get me anyway so we can go shoot something. I forget half of the stuff I need but we go to a prairie dog village and get set up. Now I have never done this and hadn't shot a lot of rifle so I was rather inexperienced. But when you make stupid mistakes right off the bat, it will take the rookie right out of you. We begin the hunt by laying on a flat area with our rifles all sandbagged up and the shooting begins. Every time we would shoot a prairie dog it seemed like another would come out. I was like a real live video game. I had never seen so much shooting in my whole life. I would shoot one and the others would drag the dead one down into a hole. We played this game for a while but not nearly as long as I would've liked. As things would have it something else came up. What came up was my scope. Yep, it smacked me square in my forehead. I take a shot and before you know it I cannot see anything, I am damn near knocked out. I get all sweaty feeling and begin to wipe at my face. The sweaty feeling was not sweat at all. It was blood, yes, blood. I had just split my head wide open on the scope of a low power rifle.

I was rather embarrassed and really didn't

feel like shooting much more and called it a day. My buddy's plan did work though. Not one thing was on my mind during that whole day. So if you are ever really stressed over things you can't change, whack your head and begin to bleed profusely. It will make it all go away.

I have hunted with that same buddy over the years and like I said earlier, if you hang around me long enough you will eventually get mad at me about something. All good things must come to an end. And for a while that friendship did end. We got cross with each other for a brief time and didn't talk. It was really sad. The guy taught me a lot about hunting and about life. We were mad about something so simple that it would only take two minutes to fix. But we refused to give it the two minutes.

So during that time I lost a hunting buddy. I worked weird shifts and was not off on the days that others were. I ended up becoming more and more of a duck hunter due to convenience. I didn't have people to go places with and didn't have a lot of places to hunt either. But duck hunting was easy. They usually flew to land on public waters and it was something I learned to do on my own. With all the gadgets, it was something I could do year round. I would work on decoys and blinds during the off season to prepare for the fall. Before you know it, I become one hell of a duck hunter.

I really become ate up with duck hunting and

shot tons of different ducks. I loved how each one was a beauty that could be hung on the wall. I have a drake of almost every duck that flies through the central flyway mounted. Each one is awesome to look at. I soon became rather involved in duck hunting but didn't have a lot of people to go with. All the people that knew me realized just how carried away I got. They didn't really want to stand out in the freezing weather or carry all the gear out to kill a few birds and then go home. So I continued to hunt alone. It was fun for me and there was no pressure from others about anything. When I would get off work I would find a water hole and go shoot some birds. Me and my dog would sit out and spend a day together every chance we got. I don't know how many ducks there have been but I promise it's more than triple digits.

I continued to hunt with some of my buddies for other animals and would bring along anyone that would come duck hunting. I had killed several animals, lots of birds and caught tons of fish with my friends, but most of the time I hunted alone. I didn't hang out with my buddies like I used to. Hunting became more of a family or alone kind of deal.

As life experiences changed me I soon realized just how much the outdoors did for me. And how much I missed the friends that showed me how to do it.

It had been a couple of years since I had spoke with some of my friends when I wrote my first book. A long lost buddy heard I wrote a hunting and fishing genre book an asked one of my friends about it. He asked the other buddy, and I quote, "What is Shannon writing a book about, hunting and fishing? The only thing he has killed was 1000 ducks and 20 friendships." I laughed so hard when I heard that, pop started coming out of my nose. After I thought about it he was more accurate than I liked. I did let life get in the way of friends. I have always done it my way, even when my way wasn't the right way.

I went right to that buddy and tried to make things right. What is sad is they weren't screwed up nearly as bad as I thought. We both chuckled about the book and rekindled the friendship, which was more like a brotherhood. It was funny to talk about how life has changed us. I was proud to let him know that I had learned a lot about the outdoors. We shared stories and made up for some lost time.

As you have seen me say several times before, the outdoors changes people. Like the old saying 'if people worried about the important things in life there would be a shortage of fishing poles.' That's about as good of a quote as there could ever be. The outdoors makes good people become simple and lose the stresses of the real world. It gives them time to get away and just enjoy what God has given us. If you have killed a friendship with a buddy, more than likely it won't take much to fix it. Especially if it was an outdoor buddy. That common bond created while chasing down wild animals never goes away.

RANDOM NAVIGATION

So it all begins on a road trip to one of my absolute favorite fly fishing holes. We are about five hours from where we are headed. I will not disclose where we went because I love this place and don't want you catching my fish. Yes, I am being a selfish ass.

I am going on this trip with a buddy who is pretty much a dry fly purest. He believes there is something sacred about catching trout on dry flies. I have fished some small farm ponds with this guy and he knows what he is doing but this is our first trip of any distance from the local ponds.

We take off to, well let's just say, the hills. Yes, we are going where the term hillbilly just means you're a native. We both are cracking jokes along the way about the hills but we are also both extremely excited to land some trout. We plug in our navigational system to give us directions and the adventure begins. We both decide that beings we are going on such a long trip we probably need some new gear. So we detour our plans a bit and go to Cabela's. We get there and we both stock up on crap we just can't live without. Hell I still have a bunch of that stuff new in the package. We get to Dallas, TX and the first thing we do is go to eat. We find this BBQ establishment where the waitresses are all half naked, wearing the least amount of clothing the law will allow. Now I have to say that if I looked like any of them that I would probably be showing it off as well. Well as fate would have it, the ugliest chick in the building happens to be our waitress. So while all the other guys in the building are enjoying their meal and a show, we are planning an exit strategy.

We finish up our meal and we head to my favorite store. Man I really think I could spend every cent I ever made in this place. We get some new fly fishing gear and my buddy stocks up on his supply of 'dry flies,' because in his eyes there is no other. Several hundred dollars later, we hit the road. We start towards hill country and the navigational system decides it has a plan, and of course we do as it tells us. Now my navigational system is just like having my girlfriend riding in the passenger seat. It barks directions and thinks it's always right when we are driving. It has this female voice that talks to you and a map that shows the way. However, Dallas/Fort Worth grows faster than most places so the navigational system is not a hundred percent accurate. That being said, we are getting on and off the interstate at really random places only to get back on again. We do this for quite some time till finally we get on a highway that the lady in the box decides will work. We drive this for several hours and are getting pretty close to our destination. The device then asks if we want to avoid unpaved roads. Neither of us have a schedule to worry about so we decide what the hell, and take the unpaved road option. So this obnoxious little voice takes us off on some road and I have no idea where the heck I am.

Now the scenery is beautiful. The trees totally cover the road like a canopy. The sun is shining through the trees and sparkling on all the vines and wild flowers that are covering everything. The place is so green and luscious that it resembles something like Ireland. Minus any leprechauns or good beer. Plus there is probably one too many people around here who loves their cousin. Eventually we get on this back road that is only a one lane. It cannot be more than eight feet wide. You cannot see anything in front, behind or beside you. The road has super sharp curves every twenty feet and everything is completely covered by greenery.

We go for a while and the lady in the box decides that she has no clue where we area at either. We have no choice but to go forward and pray we don't stumble onto anyone's marijuana field, bigfoot or whatever else lingers around in the hills. We do finally make it to a highway and the lady in the box figures out where we are again. About an hour goes by and we are at our final destination. We get a motel and get our gear organized for the morning fish. I get some of my flies together and my buddy is doing the same with his. I continue to make fun of his dry fly fishing. He says, "If you don't fish with a dry fly, you might as well fish with a minnow." I laugh at him, but I will only fish with flies that I personally have tied, so I guess I am just as strange.

The next morning we head to the water. The weather is horrible. It's cold, raining and it's cold. Oh I already said that, but anyway it's cold. He is casting his dry flies and I am trying whatever will bite. I finally get an olive bead head wooly bugger out and they start to hit. All of the sudden Mr. Dry Fly doesn't mind a subsurface fly at all. No matter how pure you believe something is, if it's not working the other options become less 'un pure.' The fishing is stinking up pretty bad and the weather hasn't improved at all either. I don't know if I have mentioned this yet but it was cold.

We struggle with the weather and finally decide that going to do something else is not a bad idea. Now we have just purchased several hundred dollars worth of gear for this trip. Gear that we did not need at all. We had everything you could imagine before we even started. Now we are leaving early anyway. We decide that this weather is not for fishing since it is cold, windy and wet. We decide that those weather elements all but speak of a duck hunt. So there you have it, our minds are set. Duck hunting it is. So our little lady in the box takes us back to Cabela's. Now Cabela's is four hours out of the way to both the place we were going and the place we were coming from. But it's cold, it's wet and that's what we want to do. So we truck there with not much excitement at all. We get to Cabela's and give the girl that works there a sob story about how bad times were and we need to exchange our stuff. She, without hesitation, lets us do just that and then gives us a friends and family discount on any other purchases. So we took that as a sign from God that we probably needed some new duck hunting gear. So we walk out with more stuff than we walked in with to return. The girl that we gave the sob story to got to see just how full of shit we were. We get back on the road and the lady in the box chips away and gets us into a really interesting place. Now before I go on any further some things are just too screwed up to make up. So believe me this is true. We have just pulled over for gas at a place that the navigational system thought was where we needed to go. We pull into the parking lot and as we pull in we start getting surrounded by people. We soon realize that we have the only vehicle in the parking lot with all four matching rims and tires and that is less than a decade old.

It looks pretty rough but, what the hell, how bad can it be? We step out of the truck and are greeted by a black man in his mid thirties. He looks and smells like he has not showered since his mid twenties. He immediately approaches us and the first thing out of his mouth was, "Man I don't want to hurt you." He further explains that his wife and kids are stranded in a car and that he needs money. Now me and my buddy both witnessed this guy get up from the curb by the dumpster, so we knew he was full of shit.

As we are walking toward the store he gets up in our face and my buddy calls him out on his bluff. My buddy just asks him if he is wanting booze. The bum then admits that booze is all he really wants. So as an honor to him for his honesty my buddy gives him a beer that we had in the cooler in the truck. Now I am not a wuss by no means but I was getting extremely nervous about this whole situation. We are in the hood of Dallas, a bum is coming to our truck and the longer we are there the more people are approaching us. So I am thinking that this is a really good time to leave. My buddy however has to pee so bad that he thinks hanging around this place for a couple minutes is worth it. We do survive the whole ordeal and my buddy gets back to the truck. As we are pulling out of the parking lot another bum takes the beer the guy just got from us and breaks it right over his forehead. So this guy who was about to strong arm us just got knocked out and had this huge gaping wound on his forehead.

My buddy didn't mind being there but thank God he didn't feel the need to be a good Samaritan and he just drove off.   We are laughing and thinking just how bad that could have been and how screwed up of a place this is, when a truck drives by. Not just any truck, a beautiful 1957 candy apple red step side. On the door of this gorgeous truck is an airbrushed picture of momma bear bent over and poppa bear doing his thing to her. I am telling you this picture was high quality. Whoever owned the truck had to have spent some money to get this done.   Like I said some things are just too strange to make up.

The next morning we go to a pond at another location that I cannot talk about and we get set up for some duck hunting. The ducks are flying in and the weather is perfect for duck hunting. It was so cold that while we were in the water it completely froze around our legs. We had to break ice just to get out.

We don't have a dog and since we were on a fly by the seat of our pants kind of hunt we have to figure out how to retrieve out birds. We find an old canoe on the pond. With the canoe is the most unique boat oar I have ever had the pleasure to use. It was an eight foot two by four with an old Texas license plate nailed to it.

So we break the ice, paddle our way to ducks and decoys we decided were worth saving. We ended up leaving several decoys out there. It was so damn cold that we figured decoys were easier to replace than our lives. We get back to the cabin to warm up and sit around telling the stories that just took place. Talk about a 'pure' kind of fishing trip turning out to be not quite so pure or even safe for that matter. All while taking directions from some lady trapped in a four inch square box is leading us on some kind of random navigation.

SANDHILLS

It all started several years ago as I was sitting at a pond duck hunting when this flock of ginormous birds flew over my blind. They landed in the field across the road. As they landed it was a sight damn sure worth watching and one that I won't forget. It was nothing at all like watching other waterfowl land. These birds had very little grace as they approached landing, actually the word 'clumsy' would be more fitting to explain how they land. But no matter how clumsy they are to watch land it is an unbelievable sight. The huge wingspan they have makes it sound and feel like you are stuck right in the middle of a windstorm. When they fly in the formation is perfect. It looks like Marines marching through the sky. But when they land they are so big and clumsy that it appears they are going to tip over and crash land into each other as they weeble wobble to the ground.

Watching these birds soon turned into an obsession, I found out that there was in fact a hunting season for these mystical creatures of the sky. I watched these birds all season long but didn't know how to hunt them. I got myself prepared for the next season. The more I watched them the more and more I could hardly wait to shoot one and of course add it to my trophy collection.

The next year seemed like it took forever to arrive but when it did, I came out in full force to hunt crane. I found a perfect spot where they had been roosting at for several days on the river. I get hidden the best I know how. It doesn't take long and the Sandhill Crane are beginning to fly over. They are getting louder as they get closer and my heart feels like it cannot handle much more. The crane are in groups of thirty and sometimes even more. They start to get close and when I think they are close enough, I jump up and Boom. Boom. Boom. I look out to where I shot and sure enough, three empty shotgun hulls is all that is out there. I did not kill a single bird. These birds were bigger than I thought and I shot way too soon at them. Either way it was over and the birds were scared off. I didn't see another bird that day. The remainder of the season kind of went the same way. That first season came and went and I didn't get a single crane. I didn't give up, I just worked harder. It began with 20 sheets of ¼" plywood and a jig saw. I made a ton of decoys and painted them to where I thought they looked pretty good. I truck along for another year and on the first hunt of the next year I set a field of decoys out.

So I am now in a field covered with decoys, where they have been landing for at least a week. I am hiding in some weeds and I can see crane coming my way. Every time they would get close to my decoy spread they would veer off the other direction. I don't know if my decoys looked that bad, or if I had so many the real birds didn't think they had room to land. Either way, they didn't do anything but make me tired setting them up and taking them down.

So I take the decoys one step further and staple real feathers on the decoys thinking that would make them look real. I was determined that would solve my problem. Nothing worked with that spread either. So two years down and I am still with out a crane. I have a spot that has been cleared in my trophy room for one and there is nothing in the spot but dust and bad memories.

By now all of my buddies have figured out that I want a crane as bad as any other creature out there. I am pretty sure at this point a crane would rate higher than an African Plains hunt in my eyes. I think more and more about what may possibly be wrong with what I am doing. The only idea I can come up with is that I need more fire power. So I purchase a Browning Pump 10 gauge. I figure a big boom for big birds, and try it again. At forty dollars plus for a box of shells I am thinking that this better work. So I go on a hunt and nothing, didn't even see a bird. I am pissed off so bad that every time I see them in the field the temptation to blast at them just comes to mind. But what kind of trophy would that be? So thank God my senses always did what was right and didn't let me stoop to being a poacher. But I am working pretty hard at shooting a bird with no luck.

One day I arrive home from yet another unsuccessful hunt. I make it to the house and low and behold if there isn't a big ass Sandhill Crane sitting dead on my front porch. I am wondering how the hell did that get there? As I am staring at this bird I get a phone call. It's my lifelong friend who asks how my hunt went. I begin to make up more excuses about why it's not my fault and that I have yet to shoot a crane. As I am giving my sob story he just breaks out laughing at me. He goes on to tell me that he doesn't understand why I am having problems killing one, and then says, "Hell I hit one with my truck driving down the road." He then starts laughing telling me he put it on my porch. I am really getting my fill of failure with these birds. I get his bird he has run over and take it to the trash. I want you to know it was hard not to take it to the taxidermist, but I could not stomach taking a bird I didn't kill. Either way, a lot of crap talk continued about how I have made decoys, spent hundreds if not thousands of dollars on crap to hunt them and still I cannot get one. But my buddy can just drive down the road and one flies right into his truck like it was on some kind of suicide mission.

As time goes on me and my body begin to realize I was growing old and slowing down. I learned that I needed to just figure out a way to make them come to me without so much damn work. I learned of a spot where they roost and where I could hide. So me and my buddy set up to shoot them. Holy crap did they ever come. Thousands fly in and we shoot our three shots, reload and shoot three more. Out of the thousands, and when I say thousands I am not exaggerating one bit, we shoot two. Yep, two. I was so excited to have shot one but could not believe that we had only shot two, one each. We go to recover the birds and they are lesser Sandhills. They are way smaller than the greaters that I had seen previously. So I am happy and sad at the same time but still determined to get one of the big ones.

During this same season I went to a sniper school for work and had got a ghillie suite for the class. I never really wore it but my buddy decides that is how we should approach the problem. So we get dressed up, go lay down in some tumble weeds and the hunt begins.

Now this afternoon was probably the coolest afternoon of my life. I got to witness some things that I probably never will again. It starts out by us laying on the bank among a bunch of tumble weeds. Let me tell you, I had them stuck all over me and had stickers in every part of my body imaginable. But we lay there and groups of about fifty birds are flying in.

They fly over us, circle around and are

landing in a field just to the East of us.

The groups continue coming in and every so often they will fly in low enough to get a shot at them. We hit about one in every ten shots we took, hell that may even be stretching the truth in our favor a bit. But we have a couple on the ground. All of the sudden huge groups of crane are flying over, by the thousands. They are coming in so fast that it sounds like a tornado and you can feel the breeze as they are flying over. The unique noise that they make has taken over the sky and I am in complete awe about what I am witnessing. As a whole are just not getting close enough to shoot at. So we are just laying on the ground freezing our asses off and looking at these huge flocks of crane flying over. When all of the sudden me and my buddy both try to talk but cut each other off. We both at the exact same time saw three White Crane.

Now for those of you that don't know what I am talking about when I say 'white crane.' I am talking about Whooping Crane. There are only about 400 left in the world and three just flew right over us. I stopped shooting for the sake of not taking a chance of hitting one of these rare treasures. We just sat and watched them fly over. They were on the left side of the V formation of the Sandhill's flying by. There were thousands of crane landing all around us but all of the sudden I didn't care about them. It was the three white ones that I was mesmerized by. I later read that evening that there are about 400 in the world. It went on to explain that the odds of winning the lottery are 1 in 13 million and the odds of seeing a wild Whooping Crane are 1 and 310 million. I don't know how accurate that data is but needless to say I felt pretty damn lucky about seeing them.

We ended up with two birds and called it a day. On the way home me and my buddy both were somewhat star struck about what we had just witnessed. So we made plans to go back out the next day with a video camera and try to get a video of them flying over. So we get home and are doing our best to prepare for the next day.

The next day I have a camera that has so much cammo netting on it that it looks like a bush. I have my ghillie suit on, which is covered in tumble weeds. My buddy decides to park his truck farther away and ride his son's bicycle about a mile to our hunting spot. I cannot help but film him as he is riding. I am laughing my ass off as this 30 something year old man is riding a child's bmx style bicycle through a field as fast as he can. He looked as if he had just stole it and was running from the police. He finally gets to the hunting spot and I am laughing so hard that I can hardly think or breathe. My buddy gets suited up and we walk to the spot where we are going to hide. With every step I take I pick up another weed or stick that hooks into my suit. I get laid up and am hoping to see the Whooping Cranes again. But we are not seeing any. I guess you don't win the lottery back to back either. So it turns out to be just a hunt. And a hunt it was, the birds were flying all over the place and we got several shots. We are not hitting them as often as we would like but birds are hitting the ground.

It gets close to shooting hours and we gather up our stuff to go home. My buddy is gonna ride his bicycle back to the truck and I am going to get the downed birds. I am laughing and telling him how he is old and gonna be out of breath and all I have to do is pick up birds. We get our gear gathered to one spot and I go after birds. There is one bird in the water, now keep in mind that the water is only about ankle deep, or so I thought. I take off knowing it is not deeper than my boots are. I make it to about five feet from the bird and I find a hole, and as you are probably figuring out, it was way deeper than ankle deep. It's about knee deep, and I learned something at that point. A ghillie suit absorbs water like a sponge. The bottom three feet of my ghillie suit are soaked and have gained a bunch of weight. My feet are freezing ass cold, but I truck on and get the bird and go after the next. While I am getting the birds picked up there are tens of thousands of crane flying in every direction above me. I always unload my shotgun so I don't screw up and do something stupid, like shoot after legal shooting hours.

So here I am in soaking wet boots in the middle of January, in a ghillie suit that is covered in tumble weeds, most of which are stuck together, and the bottom half is soaking wet. If I didn't mention this fact, it is now freaking heavy. And with every step I take they want to fall down. I get up by the next bird and as I go to pick him up he takes off running, and long legged crane can run like a bat out of hell. So here this bird goes running across this field and is running towards a major highway. All I can think of is to chase him so he doesn't get away. Plus what if he got in the highway, a bird of that size could tear up a vehicle. So I take off running as fast as I can, which is not as fast as the crane. So it is gaining on me. As I am chasing the bird we are getting closer and closer to the highway. Vehicles are driving by and the looks I am receiving are priceless. I can only imagine what the hell the people were thinking. Some huge long legged bird running through a field being chased by something that appears to be a cross between human and bush. I am covered in mud from getting the first bird, and resemble a creature out of some bayou fairy tale, coming right out of a swamp. But I am running as fast as I can. My ghillie suit is falling down, like the pants on some punk ass crack dealer, but the bird is getting tired as well and is falling down.

I run up on the bird and it is about three times bigger than the lesser Sandhill's we killed prior to this hunt. I grab hold of the bird by the neck. Something about that made the bird get a second wind. I have this bird that is between four and five feet tall by the neck. It jumps up and tries to attack me with its feet. I now am fighting a big ass bird that is kicking me and its feet are getting tangled up in my ghillie suit. I unloaded my gun earlier so I don't even have any shotgun shells to shoot him with. I take the butt stock of my shotgun and just stroke him up side the head with it and knock him out. I now have the two birds picked up and grab the next. I am carrying three big birds, my gun, camcorder and ruck bag. I am about to pass smooth out trying to walk back to the truck as my buddy is pulling up.

I am so out of breath and my ghillie suit has gained a whole bunch more tumble weeds along the foot chase with the damn psycho bird.   I approach the truck and no matter how tired he was from riding that bicycle back he sure had enough energy to laugh at my dumb ass. I sure was tired but I would love to hear all the stories from the passer bys that saw the swamp creature chasing his evening dinner through the field.

So after almost a decade I finally have both a lesser and greater Sandhill Crane, and had the wonderful opportunity to witness three endangered Whooping Cranes fly over.

DUCK OUT OF WATER

When your favorite thing to do in the fall is duck hunt, having no water just makes things kind of suck. And things kinda sucked this past duck season. I have ponds and river bottoms all over that I can hunt and every single place that I had was dry. It was a record drought and it wreaked havoc on the watersheds.

I still remained diligent and tried to go to places that I could but it just seemed more and more like a losing battle. It was horrible and nothing I did could make it better. The stats for the season were great. There were record numbers of ducks and they were having one of the best goose seasons in history. But my favorite water hole had become desert.

I had one spot that had some water but it was down to less than ten percent of where it should be. So when your favorite water hole is missing ninety percent of its water, you know you have become desperate.

My girlfriend at the time, who is now my wife, had never been duck hunting. I had explained to her just how much fun it was, how if you ever get into it, that it becomes addictive and you will be obsessed with it. She looks at me like I am insane and after the season that she got to partake in I believe she may have been right.

I see some teal on this pond and have been

checking it out for several days. I decide that we may have a shot at it. There are just a few problems. With all the water drying out, no fresh water and record heat, the oxygen in the water has all but left. When you take ninety percent of the water from a pond that leaves way too many fish in a small water hole. With way too many fish left in stagnate water, you get an odor that is worse than anything you will ever imagine.

The banks of this pond were covered in rotten dead fish. It was horrible. The smell was the worst I had ever been around, and being a cop as long as I have, I have been around some pretty funky orders. Not even dead humans in hot summer months could compare to this aroma.

So being desperate to get some birds, I decide that I can handle this and attempt to take some birds from this pond. I talk my woman into going with me. She doesn't seem all that impressed with the idea but is willing to go. So I take her to the closest sporting good store to get all the gear that she will need.

When we get to the store they don't have any female waders. They only have male sizes. Which is fine, but men's waders are not made to go around a woman's shapely ass. So we are in the aisle of the store trying to fit her into some waders. They are either way too skinny or way to long and the only ones we are finding that will work are sock footed waders. They are the kind that don't have boots attached, the bottoms are neoprene. Something you will learn if you ever try to wear neoprene is that it is slicker than snot. My wife figures this out in a very quick fashion. She is putting these waders on and they are rather tight. To get legs short enough for her she had to get in the almost midget size men waders. They are so damn skinny that no normal human can fit into them with out a struggle. But my wife is a fighter and is not going to give up. She gets the waders on part way and she grabs them at the top. She is jumping up and down to try to get them up all the way. It is a spectacle worth every second of watching. But as she is doing this she learned the lesson of slick neoprene. Her feet go above her head and lay her flat on the ground of the aisle in the sporting good store. It was getting rather amusing to watch, but I was in fear of my life if I laughed at her. I figure that would be pushing all the limits, but I couldn't hold it back. Everything she did to help her cause only made it that much worse. She ended up getting the things on, but they did not fit her right. So she asked me to help her get the waders off.

At this point in time I promise you could have stolen anything in that store that you wanted too. If there was anyone watching the security cameras I promise they were not watching anything but us. I grab her feet to pull off the waders, they start to come off along with my wife's pants. So here we are laying on the floor of a somewhat busy sporting goods store and my wife has her bare ass hanging out. We cannot get the waders off and are having one hell of a time trying to get her pants pulled back up to cover the crack. We do find a pair that fit and finish our purchase.

Then we decide to go back to do some hunting. We arrive at the place and I am absolutely positive that my wife was not impressed. You could smell the place as we were pulling up, even with the windows rolled up. I saw a few birds on the water so I told her to sneak up with me and we will try to get set up with out spooking them too much. So we are all geared up and we do the super sneaky duck hunting march up to the water. When we approach, the green wing teal all decide that even if it is the only water hole around, these two people with guns are not making it a place that they want to hang around. As they fly off we pop off some rounds and birds are falling all over the place. The hunt lasted all of about five minutes.

I am just wearing shorts and flip flops on this hunt. It's hot and I didn't want my waders on. I take off to retrieve my teal and I carry my new shotgun along with me. Now this was the first time I had taken this gun out so it was nice, shiny and new. I get it shouldered to bring with me just in case the teal fly back in. I go to pick up my birds, thinking it's no big deal to walk to where they are.

The banks of the pond are as dry as they could ever be. There are cracks in the dirt that are over an inch wide. It looks like rock hard clay with giant cracks all around in it. So I just take off across the bank to get the birds and before I know it I have sunk. It only looked dry!! In all actuality it was anything but dry. The surface of the bank was in fact dried up clay but below was the nastiest, muddiest, and damn sure the worst smelling place I think I have ever been in my life. I sank to my crotch. My new gun was now naturally camouflaged to match the surroundings due to being covered in this stinking mud. I try to get out and I fall flat on my face. I am now covered in this slimy mess and matching the new camouflage job of my shotgun. Every step I take makes it that much worse. Before long my flip flops are missing and I have to dig through the mud to find them. (They are my favorite pair). I am about to throw up. I cannot stand the smell but there is not a lot I can do about it. I am trying to move forward and I just keep falling down like a duck out of water. I finally, after about a half an hour of fighting with this nasty stuff, make my way out to get the birds. I look back at my wife and she is rather happy to see the nasty ass I just became. I think she was thinking a dose of karma had just been administered.   Either way I get our birds and start to walk back.

Walking back was just as much of a problem. There was no way to make it across the mud. I fought my way back, using low crawl on this stinking mud, and finally get to my wife. It took all I had to not ask her if she was addicted to this new hobby, because wasn't it great just like I told her? I was covered head to toe in mud, didn't have anything to wash with and it was a losing battle to try to rinse off in the pond. I tried and tried but the more I got around the water I just sank in the mud over and over again. I finally say to heck with it and just give up. I know that my truck has some baby wipes inside of it so I think I will just use them when I get back.

I get to the truck and try to get cleaned up but it was not a very successful attempt. I am not in my hunting truck. I am in my nice truck and don't want to get the mud all over everything, but if I wanted to get home I was going to have to. I now smelled as bad as the dead fish on the bank and I look like I live under a bridge. I end up stripping down to my underwear and driving home like that. It seemed like everyone I knew was on the road when I was heading home. I'm glad that none of them wanted to stop and visit.

That was my wife's first duck hunt. I am pretty certain that she was not impressed with it at all. The more we tried to hunt this season the worse it got. In all my years of hunting I have never seen such a dry mess where all the birds just flew over. The water that was around was so stagnate and had no food for the ducks to eat. So if any stopped they didn't stay long.

When I finally got home I ended up taking a shower with my gun. It was so muddy I didn't know any other way to get the mud off. It made me think back to the Army when we would have to sleep with our weapons.

This season was one to remember. There was not one thing that went right. I hope that my wife and mother nature are both more forgiving next season. There also needs to be lots of ducks, lots of water and some cold temperatures to make up for such a horrible season. The only good thing about this season was all the pre season work getting everything ready.

It will surely pay off for next year. We never even busted out the decoys. So they are all ready and set up for the next round. One thing I learned is that my wife will drag anything home if she let me come home smelling and looking the way I did that day. I guess I'm a pretty lucky guy for my wife to be my hunting partner and allow me in her house after a day out like that.

ARMY SURPLUS BULLFROGS

The other day while driving down the road I saw a piece of property for sale that brought back a ton of memories. The piece of property sat across the road from the school I grew up at. It was a small rural school out in the middle of nowhere. There was neither enough students nor enough money to keep the school open. In turn it closed down at the end of my ninth grade year. I loved that school with all my heart.

Southside School was a very small school. There were only about one hundred students from pre k through high school seniors. We were very active in sports and most of the time we barely had enough players to play. But when we played, we won. There was a sense of teamwork that I have never witnessed any other place in my life. When you need everyone you have to make it work you learn to trust those around you. Growing up in such a small school, you were friends with everyone and you learned to work out your differences. If anyone wanted to act like punk children they were dealt with and they either quit acting that way or they left. You became close with your peers too. Almost thirty years later I still hang out and talk to most all of my friends from there. There were no racial tensions, no gangs, no drama, just plain old fashioned country kids who made more with less.

Growing up without a lot of money and living in the middle of nowhere, you learned to do with what you had. We did not have cell phones, internet and it was about twenty miles to much of any store other than the local co-op. We all participated in sports and probably won more basketball games and baseball games than any other school around. We learned what work was. Our Ag classes worked every day building things or scrapping metals to make money to help the school.

After school if we were not playing sports we were usually outside doing something. We were not out raising too much hell, doing dope or any of the stuff that others did. Most of the time we were on a pond or at the river fishing. We all collected baseball cards and even our teachers took part in that hobby. They would sneak us twenty miles north to town and buy us cards when we were supposed to be in class.

We all hunted too. If they ever checked our vehicles I am certain that there would have been a shotgun in almost every one of them. But as young kids we had to keep busy, and that we did. We were always outside playing army or something similar. There was an Army surplus store that was about twenty miles away. I know that as a kid, me and my friends would always save our money and most every cent we had was probably spent there. We looked like little soldiers. In today's standards we would have been run out of school and treated as terrorist. But we were kids, having fun and doing what kids do.

One of my favorite things as a young child was dressing up in army gear and camping or playing war in the fields across from the school. One of my cousins and I were fairly close in age. During our grade school years we would stay at one another's house. We would get all dressed up and head to the fields.

If you walk about a mile or so from my cousin's house, located right beside the school, there was a field that had a small pond on it. I can think back to my first trip out there. We were dressed in green, faces painted and equipped with some of the finest military accessories that a second grader could possibly afford. We marched our happy asses down the road, calling cadence as we marched. I am sure we repeated most any line that we had heard in the military movies. We marched down the road to the field set up a camp of sorts. After all, we had just marched at least twenty minutes and needed to rest.

We would sit on our old worn out pads. Which of course some soldier had used several decades ago and used most of the life out of. But we were happy to have it. Then we would cook some of the finest food that was left over from our great grandfather's war. But we ate, and we would talk about how we were going to take over whatever nation that we were about to invade. After filling our hearts and minds full of all the made up data, we would pack back up and march forward. Over the hill and through the tall grasses we would go. Trying to avoid getting bit by snakes, bugs or whatever other kind of creepy crawlers there were. I remember on one of the walks I didn't quite escape the creepy crawlers. I was walking along and sat down to drink out of my dad's canteen. I started to itch really badly. Oh my God it was awful! I had up to that point never felt anything like it. I was wearing whitey tighty underwear and whatever it was that had attacked me sure loved the elastic bands in them. So here I am trying to play soldier and sneak up on 'Charlie' across the field. I cannot sit still for the fact that anywhere within four inches of my underwear now feels like it's on fire. I had in fact met up with my first enemy. Chiggers!! Holy crap if they didn't hurt. I didn't know what to do but stand around and scratch my crotch and deal with my cousin laughing at me. I didn't know what happened and was damn sure not going to show anyone what that heck had happened to me. I would have to take my underwear off, and there was no way in hell that anyone was going to see me with no underwear.

I ended up toughing it out and marching forward. I remember trying to march but the more I scratched the more they burned and the more they spread. I was literally bleeding by time I made it back home. I didn't quit though, I had enemies to fight.

I continue to get closer to the pond and my cousin is ahead of me. We are about to shoot the enemy with our bb guns. I was not sure who or what the enemy was but my cousin, who was a couple years older than me, had an enemy in mind and was in a mindset to kill 'em. However, his younger cousin scratching his crotch and itching so bad that he couldn't set still, was probably affecting his stalk. But he was patient and we made it to the enemy territory. The enemy territory was a swampy pond. This pond was covered in moss but shallow enough that a person could walk across it and never have water above your waistline. We got close and my cousin motioned with his hands to come forward. As I am coming forward he is motioning for me to be quiet. Now I am not talking but I am having one hell of a time trying to be still. I have this problem that has still not gone away and I have a new one too, Mosquitoes!!!! So not only am I being eaten alive at the mid section, now I have these horrible pests chewing all over the rest of my body. While blowing all of my money on Army surplus, I never thought that protecting myself from critters would help me win the war. Looking back I needed way more bug spray than I did that half of an army pup tent, especially considering that no one I played with had the other half.

But I still fought forward. I got to the edge of the pond and my cousin gets his pellet gun out and fires off a round. The war had been officially declared, and the first casualty had been suffered. Yep, my cousin had shot a bullfrog. He has his pellet gun blasting them from every direction. I am sitting in awe at the master marksmanship my cousin is displaying. I am also amazed at how big bullfrogs grow. Hell I don't guess to that point in my life I had ever seen a bullfrog. These things could eat the toads that hopped around in our front yard. We start shooting every frog we seen. This went on for a long, long time. There were dead frogs bellying up all over the pond. My cousin is in rare form and is becoming a world class killer. He has his frogs sighted in and dead before I ever saw most of them. I did kill a few but nothing like the amount he had killed.

It was super exciting and for the most part my mind was so busy that I had forgot about the man eating bugs that had taken over my underwear line. After a while we were done. We had killed all the bullfrogs that we could see. I don't know how they became the enemy but they made a great one for a young soldier. After all, they were big, so they were easy to shoot. They made lots of noise so you knew where they were, and there were tons of them. Most important, they didn't shoot back.

So now that we had won our first war, it was time to pick up the victims. I wasn't sure what was going on but my cousin was out picking up all the frogs. He took off through the stinky water and was getting mud all over. I was wondering what the hell was wrong with him. Why would he get that dirty to pick up a dead frog. But he was over excited and dedicated to get every last one of them. I stood and watched but didn't get in the water. I knew that if I did, no matter how tough of a soldier I thought I had become, that there was one thing that would always have my rear, MOM! There was no way in the world that I would ever come home covered in mud that bad. There was nothing worse than the wrath of a mad mom, especially mine. Standing just over five feet tall, that woman had an ornery side that no man, no matter his size, wanted to contend with. So I played it smart and didn't get muddy.

My cousin had gathered up all the frogs and had way more than he could carry, so I offered to help. I felt like a natural born killing machine carrying all those frogs back. I thought it would take us all night to bury the frogs that we had killed, but we killed them so I guess it was the right thing to do. We marched our happy little selves back to his house. We are flat wore out, and running late. No matter how hard I tried to not get my mom mad at me, I had failed. I still ended up covered not only in mud, but frog blood and mom was asking why I was scratching my crotch? Talking about an itchy crotch to your mom, when you're in the second grade, was something that I damn sure wanted to avoid. So here we are staring at our parents who were staring back at us. They were not looking at us as proud as we were looking at them. My mom is telling me to get my ass in the car, and I am trying to tell her I need to help my cousin burry the frogs. Everyone begins to laugh. I had no idea what they were laughing at, but it was way better than being in trouble.

I asked what is so funny? My cousin tells me that he is not going to bury anything. He tells me that these frogs are dinner. Now I have no clue what my facial expression was at this point, but I can guarantee that it was something similar to an 'oh shit' look. I thought he was screwing with me. But as I stood there and watched him clean the frogs, I realized he wasn't. He went through each and every frog, pulling the legs off of them like they were chickens. He would rinse them off and place them in baggies. All I could think about was that my cousin must have smoked his breakfast. There was no way in hell you were going to get me to eat a frog, hell I don't even eat fish. As young as I was, I could not imagine that anything good could come from a frog. After all, if you touch one you will get warts.

I stood around and watched my cousin. Then he said he was going to cook some. I had to see it. My mom gave in and allowed me to stay for a while. When my cousin would throw them in the frying pan, they would jerk and jump like they were alive. I watched that a couple of times, which was plenty. If there ever was a chance to get me to eat one of them, he sure blew that chance all to hell. But he ate them and said that they tasted like chicken. It seemed to me that all strange food that people ate, tasted like chicken. So I still was not impressed. At the end of the day it was just two country kids growing up in the 'real' world. Sheltered from all the scary bad things that kids today face. It was fun playing Army. Even if I got chiggers and had to eventually drop my whitey tighty undies so my mom could see what had been eating me. I never ate any frog legs and still to this day I have never tried them. I think I would, just to settle the curiosity set in my mind so long ago. Hell I may just want to see if they really do taste like chicken.

I guess that's the one thing that I love most about living in the same place most of my life. Driving down the road and looking at some old field, with a body of water that now appears way smaller and closer to the road than I ever remembered, tosses up a memory in my mind of the war with the Army surplus bullfrogs.

I'VE GOT BUGS

I have learned that life is a big circle. If you don't believe me look at your own life and others around you. What comes around goes around. Everything we do is for a reason, even if it takes years till we find out what that reason is. I hear people all the time say it was a waste of time for something they did, but our past is what makes our future.

As a young adult I wanted to make it big. I was not really certain how I was going to make it but I promised myself I would. I would try most anything I could imagine to make a buck. I didn't have a purpose and damn sure had no rhyme or reason for most of the things that I did. I also wasn't happy doing what I was doing. I didn't realize that happiness is doing something that you love to do, not just what pays the bills. So all my life I worked doing things I didn't like. But after a few major changes in my life, I decided I too was going to chase a dream.

I will start this out with a quote. "When I was 5 years old, my mother always told me that happiness was the key to life. When I went to school, they asked me what I wanted to be when I grew up. I wrote down 'happy.' They told me I didn't understand the assignment, and I told them they didn't understand life." --John Lennon. This quote fully sums up my attitude about life.

This story will take us from the time when I was seventeen, and as I said everything comes full circle, so we will end up in present time. I love the outdoors more than anything, but growing up I never figured a guy could make a living playing outside. I was told by a man I really looked up to that I should always make my hobbies profitable. That never made much sense to me until I became an adult.

After going through women like most men go through boots and having to walk away from everything to take care of a dying parent, I soon realized that 'happy' was all I really did want. I also knew that if I could make it doing something that interested me, every day work would not be nearly as miserable. So in trying to figure out the thing that I probably loved to do the most, it hit me like a brick. Hell, it has to be fly fishing.

Fly fishing is the one hobby I have that can consume me. Ever since I was a young child I loved the mystery of fly fishing. I became wrapped up in tying flies every chance I had. It made me appreciate nature more than ever before. A walk in the woods was never the same for me after learning to tie flies. I was looking in the trees, on the ground and trying to find some sort of material that I didn't have. Before long I had pounds of feathers, that doesn't sound like too much, but think to yourself just how many feathers are in a pound.

I took fly tying classes and went on fly fishing trips all over. I set it in my mind that I wanted to mount one of every fish I caught on my fly rod. I wanted to make a place where people could come look at the fish and realize that any fish could be caught by anyone with a fly rod.

The main problem I realized when I started fly fishing was that I lived in Southwest Oklahoma. If you want people to look at you funny, go asking where to fly fish in Southwest Oklahoma. There is a stigma in people's eyes that fly fishing is a hobby for old rich snobby men in the streams of Colorado. I too at one point had that same thought. Hell I grew up in Golden Colorado. I had seen those men with the funny hats fishing in the creeks with my own eyes. But I was fascinated with it. I would come home from summers in Colorado with my dad and want to continue my hobby at home in Oklahoma. But there were no place to really fly fish or to get materials.

I met a couple of people who also seemed very interested in fly fishing. They would ask questions about it and I would teach them what I knew. If someone was going on a trip somewhere I would tie up some flies for them and before long I was putting on fly tying classes. So when me and my wife decided to start up our new business, it was a no brainer. We already had one. We just needed to make what we already had grow.

Now this is the part that makes me different from most people. This was not about money. Of course I wanted to make some money with my business. After all, if you have a business that doesn't make money it's not going to stay in business. But I knew a fly shop was by no means, a get rich scheme. Truthfully I didn't really care. Hell, I had already pissed more money away on stupid stuff in my life, than any one man should be able to.

I was there. I was going to make my hobby something that could spread my passion of fly fishing to others. If there is one business in Southwest Oklahoma that would not have much competition it was a fly shop.

But what would I call it? As my wife and I discussed numerous ideas, once again I was hit by a brick. Like I said, everything comes full circle. One of the most insane ideas in my life finally had a reason. It was catchy and after doing some research it was mine for the taking. No one had registered the name so I knew it was a sign from God.

This crazy idea started when I was just barely out of high school. I was a bit big for my britches and thought I was a mastermind in business. I had been doing a lot of landscaping for people and had become very interested in organic gardening. I read books and articles on organic gardening and realized that nature has a way to take care of most anything. We didn't have internet back then so I read a lot of magazines. In the back of one magazine I read about beneficial insects. Which was right up my alley. So I ordered some ladybugs.

This company was selling them and stated that the ladybugs will protect your plants from other harmful insects. So I had to order some. I made on order for a thousand ladybugs. They arrived in a small baggie made of burlap. The directions stated to put them in the refrigerator and they would basically go to sleep for extended periods of time. When you were ready to use them, all you had to do was get them out and let them go. When they warmed up they would wake up and be ready to work.

I never thought it would work but I had to try it. After all, if I had all organic plants coming out of my green house then I had a marketing tool. I let my lady bugs loose and they took over my green house. Hell I had never seen such an improvement in plant quality. I had no more aphids, the worst bugs for eating plant leaves in my area. It was working and other people were acting interested.

I did some more research and realized that the more bugs I bought, the cheaper they were. I also knew that the baggies they came in could be sewn up by my mother and we could sell lady bugs on our own.

I will never forget the day that my 72,000

ladybugs showed up at the house. I still lived at home with my parents, so I had to ask mom if I could put these bugs in her refrigerator. Mom never really knew what to think of my crazy ideas but she supported them all. She knew if I was doing stuff like that, I wasn't out partying and doing the bad things a lot of the other kids ere doing.

Now 72,000 ladybugs sounds like a whole bunch, but they fit in a gallon container. We decided that we would divide them into bags of 1000. Mom made little baggies that had my name and phone number on them. We put them in the fridge and stored them until we had a place to sell them. Packaging these was something that took some getting used to. I can't quite explain the way it feels sticking your hand into a container of 72,000 ladybugs. Nothing can quite compare to a few hundred thousand legs moving up and down your arm. It's a feeling that will make you scratch yourself for days trying to get them off, long after they have been gone. Either way it was something that needed to be done so we could get these bugs out on the market.

I have to laugh thinking about this. In order to package them in the house I convinced my mom that these bugs were asleep. And they were asleep when we started. By time we measured out groups of a thousand the little critters started moving around. Before you know it my mom's house had been taken over by ladybugs. They were everywhere. I don't think I will ever live that down. I never got to package bugs in the house after that day.

We started to package the bugs outside instead. To this day I think the town I live in has one of the largest ladybug populations around. There are times in the fall that you can open the door and see thousands of them gathered up on the screen door. We figured out a system to measure them and before long I had a bug packaging factory to beat all others.

I still had to figure out how to sell these critters. I wasn't sure if there was anyone else out there, that was as easy to convince as I was to buy a bunch of bugs in a bag. But I was damn sure willing to find out. The more I asked the more I found that everyone wanted bugs to protect their gardens. So I would order more and more. Before long I know that I went through literally a couple of million ladybugs.

Every green house within a hundred miles was buying my ladybugs. I say that. I don't know where they all were, but if I knew about a green house, I had talked them into buying my bugs.

I still had not come up with a business name for this whole ordeal. I was getting pretty cocky about how much money I was making off of these bugs, all while doing very little work. I figured it was time to take this show to the next level. I wasn't sure how to get to the next level but I was gonna figure it out.

I had found a large department store chain that wanted to carry my lady bugs to sell to their customers. The greenhouse employee told me that I would need to talk to their general manager. The manager explained to me I needed to go to their corporate office and present my business plan presentation to the head people in charge.

Now by no means am I even close to being politically correct about anything that I have ever done. This day was not any different. I had to drive two and a half hours to the corporate office to meet with the big shots. I don't have a business plan set up and I am as nervous as a hooker in church. But I go to this office with my little baggies, no business name and no plan at all. Hell I had no idea what a business plan even was at this stage of life. I get to the welcome area and tell the receptionist that I have an appointment to sell ladybugs. The lady gave me this 'lost in the head light' look. She laughs at me and tells me that the office I need to go to is down the hall, last door on the right. She is looking at me like I am crazy. I have no paperwork, dressed in blue jeans and a t-shirt and have only one of my homemade packages of lady bugs in my pocket.

Every second that goes by the more nervous I am getting and the more I am realizing that I have no business being at this place. I had made it this far so there was no way that I was going to turn back now. Here I am a seventeen year old kid, walking down to the office and I can hear my stomach growling at me as my nerves had met their limit. I am sweating so bad that my armpits are literally wet on my t-shirt. I am trying to think of what I needed to say when I got into the office but nothing is coming to mind. I thought I was going to break down and cry. I was trying to make it to the big leagues in business with sweaty armpits. I have the shakes and my presentation consists of a little hand sewn baggie my mommy made. I keep thinking I should save myself the embarrassment and turn my dumb ass around while you still can. But something inside me would not let me. So I finally get to the office and the door is wide open. I bet it took me ten minutes to get the courage to turn that corner and walk in. When I finally do, Nothing!! There wasn't even anyone in the office.

I get into this giant office and I see a picture of a guy, probably the owner of the office, standing with president Bill Clinton. I was fascinated, and could not resist looking around. Hell all I could think about was that someday I would have an office of my own that was like this. Before you know it my emotions had taken over and I got a brain fart of an idea. I went and sat in the man's chair. I don't know what I was thinking but I got caught up in the moment and after all he wasn't there so I made myself at home. I sit in this giant chair and kick back pretending it's my office. The chair is super comfortable and one thing leads to another and now I catch myself putting my feet on the man's desk. I just cannot seem to get enough and before you know it I am digging in his desk drawer. As I open the drawer I see that he has some cigars. I have never smoked anything so I have no clue what a fine cigar is if it was looking me in the eye, but I can tell you these were fine cigars. As I am sitting in this chair, feet kicked up on some guy's desk with this cigar in my hand acting like I am big shit, guess what? Yep you guessed it, he walked right in on my stupid ass.

Now I may have only been seventeen but I knew when I had stepped in shit. By the look of this guy, I was sure he was about to verify my assumptions. I was quick on my feet and before he could ever get one word out I jumped right up out of his chair, threw his cigar on the floor and reached my hand out to shake his. Instead of damage control, all I could say was, "Hi, I'm Shannon Olson and I've got bugs!!!"

I had immediately turned this game around, and he was the one in shock. He even laughed out loud at me. Then told me to get the hell out of his chair and sit down. He taught me some things that day. First, that I was nowhere ready to be supplying his business with a product, and that I needed to do some pre planning on any future ideas that I may have. He did stress to me this and I quote, "Boy have you got one set of balls." So at the end of the day I left with my sweaty t-shirt, my pocket of bugs and my neutered 'set of balls.'

I will never forget that day as long as I live and I bet that man never will either. I cannot believe he didn't call the cops on me but thank God he didn't. I did figure out a name for my ladybug business. That's when 'I've Got Bugs' became set in my mind. That ladybug idea fizzled out. I sold all the bugs, which reproduced and put me right out of business. Every greenhouse had their own replenishing supply of bugs that I had sold them. So I eventually threw in the hat and decided to come up with some other get rich quick scheme.

Time went on and I decided that the one way to make it in life was to have a job. Twenty years I finally see the reason for that one event in my life. I mean hey, what a catchy name for a fly shop. So we got t-shirts, wooden nickels and all the other business advertisement stuff made. I then begin to make my passion of fly fishing spread to others. To this day it is funny to see the look on peoples face when they read 'I've Got Bugs' on something.

The best story of that was one day when I am at a training for my real job, which is an investigator for the sheriff department. I am taking a lunch break from this class, which happened to be a sexual crimes investigation class. My wife pulls out in front to pick me up to go eat. In the rear window of my pick up is a sticker   decal   of   our   business   website 'www.ivegotbugs.com.'

As my wife is walking by one of the other cops in the class looks at her and says, "You've got bugs?" Before I could get any kind of word in edge wise my wife responds back with, "Yep, but I got a cream for that. " She just walked away afterwards, not explaining one thing. That guy just gave me the strangest look and walked the other way. I laughed so damn hard that I couldn't stand it. So there you have it, an example of life's full circle. Some twenty years later I am still turning heads with my business name.

But now instead of blurting it out, we are branding everything we can with I've Got Bugs. Hoping that we can reach as many people as possible to share the wonderful world of fly tying and fly fishing with them.

BOAT OF THE BEAST

I was once told that every time a boat is purchased two fools meet, one for selling his boat and the other for buying it. After a lot of personal experience I have to say I truly and one hundred percent agree. Any man who loves the outdoors thinks in his mind that he needs a boat. I know this for certain because I am one of those men. As I write this, I have three boats and want another.

I have also learned that there are two kinds of boats, those that have left you stranded on the lake, and those that will leave you stranded on the lake. I have been involved in several incidents on the water with boats, from little ones to large ones. I have sunk a couple of boats and damn sure have paddled my way back to shore more than once.

As a young child and now an adult, I have never truly learned how to swim. I can paddle across the water and all that jazz, but I cannot go under water without holding my fingers over my nose. I don't know why I cannot, but I cant. I still to this day cannot figure out how to do it. This will be important to remember.

I have a buddy. This buddy is fun to be around and you are guaranteed a story every time you are around him. I will tell a short little story about him so you get a true feeling and understanding of just how he is. One day I get a phone call from this friend. I am not going to tell you his name because it wouldn't surprise me if he had warrants. But this friend calls me and it's late at night. He is in somewhat of a state of panic and this is how it goes.

Him: "Man, I need your help, I don't know where I am."

Me: "How the hell do you not know where you are?"

"I don't know. I was in Stillwater at the bar with some friends and now I don't know where I am."

So I tell him to go ask someone where he is and I would come get him if his friends had left him.

"That's the problem Shannon. I am in my underwear, and I can't find my clothes. I am by a highway under some sign at a gas station."

Now I am laughing so hard that I cannot even understand him anymore.

I tell him he needs to at least go ask the clerk where he is, because he is going to get in trouble sitting in his underwear in front of some random gas station.

He says he will go inside and ask and then call me back. I am now up thinking I am now and going to have to go get my buddy, who may be in jail by then. I can tell by his voice that he is either still drunk or very hung over. I am waiting for the phone to ring to see where the hell he is. I can't help but wonder how the hell do you end up at some random gas station in your underwear with just a cell phone?

He calls me back, and sounds somewhat panicked but even he is now laughing. He tells me that not only is he in his underwear, but whoever dropped him off died his hair red like a clown and left him in Amarillo, Texas.

I am laughing so damn hard that I can barely breathe. We figured a way to get him home but now that I think about it I never heard the rest of the story about who or why he got dropped off.

So back to the original story. This buddy just has a hard time acting any kind of normal and has absolutely no fear of anything. He also has no fear of people that have fears.

We decide to go fishing one day in my little john boat. He realizes I can't swim and is screwing with me. He keeps standing up in the boat rocking it all over and it takes on water. He sits back down and we scoop the water out of the boat. I have a couple of thousand dollars worth of fishing gear in my boat and he thinks it's funny to watch me about shit my pants each time he gets water in the boat. I am sitting there nervous as can be all the while thinking of how I could kill him without getting in trouble. As we get out in the middle of this large pond that is very deep he does it again.

This time the boat takes on a bunch of water and he looses his balance and falls into the pond. He is bobbing up and down trying to get back into the boat. As he is grabbing for the boat I am trying to get to the center, because it is off balance and about to flip over. As I move all of my gear falls out of the boat. I am doing everything I can to stay in the boat and to keep it up right. I end up failing at both. I too end up in the water sinking alongside all of my fishing tackle and boat. I am panicking, cannot swim and my boat is sinking. I paddle the best I know how back to shore. My buddy is trying to salvage what gear he can and to get the boat before it goes all the way to the bottom.

Now I have no clue how he did it, but my buddy got most of my gear and recovered my boat. The reason I have no clue is because I was too busy paddling. If I didn't paddle my happy ass to shore I would have been fish food left in the bottom of the pond.

I promised myself to never go in a boat with him again. I also learned that you just simply cannot trust being an any method of transportation with him. I don't know how he has survived at all.

After that day I decided that I needed a bigger boat, one that would be safer. Plus I would make it where it would float if it ever did tip over. I looked around for a while and before long I found a nineteen foot fish and ski combo boat. I didn't have a lot of money to buy a new one so I thought a fixer up would be the way to go. I found a boat with no interior, just a hull and a motor that was about twenty five years old. I looked ok and I thought I could surely fix it up. The only thing I questioned was the tag number on the boat had the numbers 666 in it. I am not superstitious but that made me worry a bit.

I was scared to death to sink again, so I decided that I would foam every inch of this boat. There would not be one void that was not filled with foam before I was finished. I worked every afternoon for a whole summer and got this boat looking great. I had foamed it so if it broke into a hundred pieces on the water that all hundred pieces would float. I built all new steering, reworked the motor, all new flooring and electronics. I was proud of this old ugly boat. I finally got my ship ready for the water. I decided to have a buddy bring his boat to the lake just in case something went wrong.

So we are at the lake. I take the boat out and she is doing great. Hell after twenty minutes with my project boat I was pretty impressed with how my boat was running. We are riding around and decide that we should race our boats against each other. So we line them up at one end of the lake and my boat is flat kicking the hell out of my buddy's boat. I go to turn around and see him headed towards my boat. He begins to wave his hands at me. I am not real sure what the heck he is doing. I am just looking at him and thinking he is playing with me, but before I could react he drives his boat right smack into the side of mine. It hits hard and I am sure that I may have peed as I stand there watching the gap close as he rams right into me. I look at my buddy and he is laughing so hard he is crying. We both just shake our heads as we survived this t-bone accident on the water. Neither one of our boats sustained any damage. My buddies steering cable had busted and he was waving to get me to move out of the way. I didn't understand what he was doing. I guess I thought he was doing the 'look no hands' driving game.

We finished the day on the water and I was super proud of how well my project boat had done. I was ready to go to the lake every chance that I got, and that I did. I have never had so many awkward moments in any vehicle or other mode of transportation as I have with that boat of the beast.

If there were big snakes around they would come to that boat. Any crazy moment that could happen did happen with that boat. One time I was at the lake taking my boss fishing. We are trucking around and this snake comes swimming up. I am telling you that this thing was insanely huge. If there really is a loch ness monster, I saw it that day. I get so damn nervous and scared of this snake in the water that I end up jumping out of a perfectly good boat (that the snake could not get into). I land in the shallow water where the snake was and run to shore. That, with several other reasons, probably made my boss wonder what the hell he was thinking when he hired me.

But I wasn't always fishing. I loved to water ski and did my share of that behind the beast as well. And just as with fishing on the water the beast would not allow a normal day of skiing either. One time me and my ex wife were at the lake. She had never drove the boat so she wasn't really sure how to. But I am skiing and she is driving I get in the water with my skis and tell her to go. She is nervous about driving for the first time and just barely eases the gas. She is not giving the boat enough power to get me up on the water. Now I cannot swim for shit, so I am having a hard time in the water and am motioning for her to go faster. This was the only time in our marriage she ever listened. She gives the boat gas, every bit of gas it had. I am standing there waiting to slowly get lifted up on the water when things go very bad.   I am standing there barely holding on to the rope and it tightens up so fast that I cannot control it. I end up airborne right into the boat. I don't really know how it happened, if I got catapulted into the boat or if it just tight lined me into the boat. Either way I was not in control of the rope and it damn near broke my leg. I never tried to ski with her driving again.

As life usually deals changes, I ended up

getting a divorce. I am not a selfish person, but I have a hard time sharing some things and a wife is one of those things I don't share. So I had to trade her off. I learned at this point that women are like pickups and if they start to give you problems, you have to trade them in. So that's what I did. But doing that cost me more money than I had, or could come up with, so I had to sell the beast.

So I sell this boat off to my uncle. He had it for a year or so but didn't get to use it much. My uncle had to move and he offered to sell me my boat back. I could not resist getting the beast back. Like I said at the beginning of the story, two fools met, him for selling it back and me for buying it.

I kept the thing around but working two jobs, being in the Army National Guard and college didn't really give me a whole lot of time to go to the lake. So with all that life gave me, I never took the boat out. And before long I didn't have an interest anymore. I no longer hung around with any of the people that I did when I went to the lake, so it was just sitting in the driveway. A buddy of mine wanted a boat and he had a bunch of traps and fly fishing stuff. I thought that would make a good trade, so we traded. If you noticed not a lot of money ever switches hands with me and my friends, we horse trade most everything among ourselves. But we make the trade and he starts to work on the boat. He gets her all in top notch shape and takes it to the lake. Low and behold if this boat, that I told him was super dependable when I had it, is now stranded on the water. This buddy of mine who traded the boat has always been good to me, so I felt awful.

We end up getting the boat to shore and start to work on it, trying to figure out what is wrong with the boat. We cannot tell if it isn't getting fuel or fire. So we decide to start doing some checking. One day we are at his house working on the boat. We have a tub of water for the motor to run in to keep the water pump full. We have left the hose running in the tub so it doesn't get empty from the boat. We get the boat to fire up and it spits and sputters for a few minutes and then dies. I had just purchased this high dollar tool to check the spark in a spark plug wire. Now keep in mind that I am not much of a mechanic so I don't really have a clue about some things. My buddy realizes this and decides to get even with me for screwing him on the boat. So he tells me to put the spark plug tester on top of the coil to see if it has a spark. I don't really see a reason why I shouldn't. I am trying to be helpful so I place my little pencil sized tool right on top of the coil of the motor. My buddy turns his head and gets down low in the boat to where I can hardly see him. I am standing in about four inches of water that has flooded over from the tub for the motor. I place the pencil sized tool on top of the coil and he fires the boat off.

Now I am one hundred percent positive that if my buddy told this part of the story it would be way funnier than I can give it justice. I have no clue how many amps or volts or whatever the hell a coil produces but I can promise you one thing. There is not a human in the world that can stand in four inches of water with that much juice running through his body. I know this, from experience. WOW! I have never in my life felt so lit up. I have touched hot wire fences, been tazed in training as a police officer and neither one can compare. I don't know if the water helped out or if that sucker just made that much juice. All I know is my little hundred dollar tool went airborne. My watch left a burning sensation around my wrist and my mouth was sagging as if I had just had a stroke.

I try to talk to my 'so called' buddy who is laughing so hard that he literally cannot talk. Hell for that matter he can barely function. I am certain that he will never forget getting me that day. All I can do is think to myself that I am going to get him back come hell or high water. But it won't be right away, because at the current moment I was stunned and wasn't able to do much of anything about anything.

Anyway, that day came and went but the laughs never stopped. If I bring that story up today, he will just stop whatever he is doing and begin to tear up from laughing so hard. As he is laughing he throws his hands up in the air and screams like a little girl. I guess that is what I did when this whole event took place. I don't honestly know. He could make up anything and I would have to believe it because I was somewhat incapacitated during the whole event.

Times like that really make me wonder why the friends I have keep me around, and vice versa, why do I keep them around? Sometimes I feel like I am the retard they keep around so they have someone to laugh at. But as I say over and over, everything comes full circle, and my buddy got his dose of Karma from the beast. Yep, he finally gets the boat going and is out on the lake fishing and playing around. He calls me to join him but I am out of town and I thank God for that.

Later I get a phone call from my buddy who thinks it's funny to shock the holy hell out of his friends. He tells me, " I get it, you are just really patient, yep, you were trying to kill me." He has this nervous sound in his voice as if something just happened, but while he is talking to me he is laughing so hard I can barely be understand him. The longer he talks the more I am understanding that the boat of the beast has struck again. The more he goes in to the story I began to put a picture in my mind of what took place.

He has the boat out in the water and is going

along when it starts to slow down. The motor is working fine but losing speed. He gives it more gas and then hears a loud cracking sound. When he looks back the rear end of the boat, the part that holds the motor on, has cracked and is separating from the rest of the boat. This is allowing the boat to fill with water and the motor is barely dangling on. He tells me that he is gunning the boat as fast as it can go, hoping to get to shore before it sank.

I felt bad that the boat was a lemon. I guess sitting so long, the boat had all but fallen apart. I figured that if a boat was almost going to sink, it couldn't have happened to a better guy. Especially after the whole 'sparky' event. We figured out that the motor was ok, but the boat had been full of water and that's why it couldn't go. All the foam I had put in the hull of the boat had rotted and soaked up all the extra water that was coming in through cracks. That weighted the boat down so much that no motor would be able to make that thing go. I look back and laugh at the boat story every time I think of it. I enjoy the story more and more each time my buddy tells it. I am certain that he gets more animated and screams a little louder each time he mimics how I responded to all the juice. All I can say is I am glad that the boat marked with the number of the beast is no longer with us. I said I was not superstitious before, but after so many incidents with that damn boat I have to say it's more than just a coincidence.

ABOUT THE AUTHOR

Shannon is originally from Golden, Colorado, but has spent most of his years in a small town in Southwest Oklahoma. He continues to live on the same block he did as a kid. He now resides there with his wife, two daughters and his bird dog, Trout.

He continues to hunt, fish and have numerous new stories to add to the collection. Even though daily work in law enforcement remains he still spends his time with family and passing on his love for fly fishing through ivegotbugs.com.

Shannon proudly uses and abuses the following:

IGTS – Your go to computer guys.
919 N. Main Street
Altus, OK 73521
580-480-4700
www.igtechs.com

Baker Boys Turkey Calls
2808 London St.
Vernon, TX 76384
www.bakerboysturkeycalls.com

Well Hung Taxidermy
618 E. Baseline Rd.
Tipton, OK 73570
www.whtaxidermy.webs.com

Pence Shorthairs
Elmer, OK 73539
Jerimypence@yahoo.com

Badlands Tactical Training Facility
408 N. Simpson
Grandfield, OK 73546
www.badlandstactical.org

I've Got Bugs – All your fly fishing needs.
Elmer, Ok 73539
580-481-0524
www.ivegotbugs.com